The Empty Nest Discover Your New Life Focus

Supporting you through loneliness and sadness to a plan of renewing friendships, reconnecting with your partner, rediscovering the joys of life, and becoming the thriving, happy woman you deserve to be.

Dani Lai MacGregor

DJM Business Services LLC

© Copyright Dani Lai MacGregor 2022 - All rights reserved.

The content contained within this book may not be reproduced, duplicated or transmitted without direct written permission from the author or the publisher.

Under no circumstances will any blame or legal responsibility be held against the publisher, or author, for any damages, reparation, or monetary loss due to the information contained within this book. Either directly or indirectly. You are responsible for your own choices, actions, and results.

Legal Notice:

This book is copyright protected. This book is only for personal use. You cannot amend, distribute, sell, use, quote or paraphrase any part, or the content within this book, without the consent of the author or publisher.

Disclaimer Notice:

Please note the information contained within this document is for educational and entertainment purposes only. All effort has been executed to present accurate, up to date, and reliable, complete information. No warranties of any kind are declared or implied. Readers acknowledge that the author is not engaging in the rendering of legal, financial, medical or professional advice. The content within this book has been derived from various sources. Please consult a licensed professional before attempting any techniques outlined in this book.

By reading this document, the reader agrees that under no circumstances is the author responsible for any losses, direct or indirect, which are incurred as a result of the use of the information contained within this document, including, but not limited to, — errors, omissions, or inaccuracies.

Contents

Introduction		V
1.	Understanding Empty Nest Syndrome	1
2.	Consequences of the Empty Nest Syndrome	14
3.	Risk factors	22
4.	Stages of Empty Nest Syndrome	29
5.	Family Dynamics: The natural Family Cycle	43
6.	Stretch your old wings plan	57
7.	Allow your children to become adults	60
8.	You are much more than a mother	75
9.	Take care of your feelings	83
10.	Fall in love with being alive	92
11.	Renew your friendships or make new ones	96
12.	Improve your career	100
13.	Fill Your Life With Meaningful Things... Especially if You're Single	103

14. Who is that man?	108
15. Making a life together	114
16. Look after your personal well-being	119
Leave a 1-Click Review!	124
Conclusion	126
Also By Dani Lai MacGregor	129
Resources	130

Introduction

" Standing alone at the top of the stairs; she breaks down and cries to her husband, Daddy, our baby's gone."- She's Leaving Home, The Beatles(1967).

One day you wake up, looking at your favorite place in the house, only to find it empty. The children have grown up and flown the nest. Many people don't understand this feeling and think I am overreacting or some sort of crybaby because I have kids, but they are an essential part of my life. This emptiness is a real thing that happens after a child graduates from high school or moves out on their own for college. The empty nest is a transition phase for the family and can be very scary.

Many people fail to understand this phase, so they try to stop it by finding more things for the kids to do, more stuff to buy, and more activities for them to do. Kids have told me that they think their parents are in denial and don't want them moving out on their own. What gives? It's like waiting for my mom to die so I can get married.

What I've learned is to realize that mom's greatest fear of the empty nest is: What is your purpose now? Is there something else you should be doing? But she doesn't ask this question because she can't bear to hear the answer. I have heard from many mothers that they are afraid to leave their kids because they think, "What if I make a mistake and these kids don't turn out okay?" This unfounded fear is like not leaving the house without lipstick or mascara on. It's more of an essential human function for survival rather than a sign of abandonment or lack of value for one's children.

The other option is that it's all about control. The parent is afraid that their kids will leave, and they want to stop them. This is a good example of "attachment theory," where the adult fears losing control. If you are living in denial, it's because you are not quite ready to let go and embrace change. Perhaps your child has decided that college life is not a good fit for them, which means it's time for them to move out on their own. Do you yell at them and make them feel bad for what they have chosen to do? I can assure you that is the absolute worst thing you can do. Ultimately, it's best to embrace it and start to appreciate what's going on. It's all about awareness- being aware of your instincts and feelings as a parent.

The stage of the empty nest is all about change. We must ask ourselves: "What is happening to my marriage now? Will it still be happy?" This will shift from being a parent-child relationship to a more adult-adult relationship. Do we even know how to talk to each other anymore? On rare occasions, the empty nest will cause you to re-evaluate your life and who you are as a person. Parents need to be open-minded and look at positive ways of dealing with this phase of life. An honest conversation with your partner about where you are going from here can go a long way toward resolving any misunderstandings.

Reading this book will help you to:

- Understand the empty nest and what it means to the family unit.

- Feel less fear around this phase of life.

- Accept change as a natural progression of life. It's worth it!

- Rediscover yourself, being more capable than just a mother. You will find support and tools to lead a meaningful and happy life after your kids have moved out.

It's important to talk about these things again because all kids need a positive role model at some point in their life. If you don't discuss these things again, they will just stay on the shelf and get buried. You need to be able to talk about these things face to face again without the kids or your child being a third party and getting hurt if you say something wrong. When it's all said and done, your child may leave the nest, but will they remember you? This is a good question, especially in their 20s or 30s. The key is to be involved again in a positive way.

Believe it or not, an empty nest results in a better life. The empty nest is freeing your life and marriage. Enjoy time alone or with friends, maybe even vacationing out of the country. Perhaps you will find a hobby or join a club or something. You are no longer beholden to your kids, so you can live your life in search of new hobbies and social circles! It's better than sleeping all day long! Don't get me wrong; it could be hard on you if they live at home again once they graduate. Take these emotions seriously and make time to analyze them. It would help if you talked about them with your partner, too, because there could be some resentment from one of you towards the other child for staying at home after graduation versus moving out on their own.

The difficult part about getting a spouse to feel comfortable about this stage is that it's not a physical ailment, so sometimes it is hard to come up with solutions. But the emotional aspect of life after children are finished with school is challenging, and you need emotional support. It's important to ensure you have support from others facing similar challenges so you don't feel alone.

You will need this book if you feel dejected from the departure of all your children from home; you cannot find a way to pick yourself up from feelings of sadness, emptiness, loneliness, and lack of meaning and purpose in your new sudden position in life; also if you are facing loneliness and an emotional void if single, or facing the considerable challenge of being alone with your partner without knowing how to be together if it doesn't involve being

THE EMPTY NEST DISCOVER YOUR NEW LIFE FOCUS

there for the kids. You will find ways to fix or relaunch your love life.

Chapter One

Understanding Empty Nest Syndrome

"Not all parents and caregivers experience the Empty Nest Syndrome, but those who do often describe it as "bittersweet." It combines the melancholy of suddenly living alone, with the intrigue of finally having time for yourself." -The bittersweet empty nest

- **What's an Empty Nest?**

The empty nest is a time in your life when your children have mostly grown up, are off to college, or have left home for their own place. The empty nest is a common theme in literature and movies of the parent who says goodbye to their last child going to college, moving out, or being deployed in the military. The empty nest is also a time when parents can look forward to having more time for themselves, their work, and their friendships. Our culture often portrays the empty nest as a negative event, sometimes as a crisis that brings sadness and loneliness to middle-aged couples. However, time spent alone after the kids leave home is one of the most positive times in life.

• Defining the Empty Nest

In this empty nest stage, parents experience a sense of freedom and a release from the daily responsibilities of raising children. It's an exciting time in life, the end of one chapter and the beginning of another. The empty-nest stage occurs when your children reach adulthood and leave home for education or employment. Other factors that influence this stage include death, divorce, and illness, resulting in living alone and bringing grandchildren into your home growing up.

• The Empty Nest Syndrome

Empty Nest Syndrome is a term that encompasses feelings of anxiety and depression experienced by some parents in the post-child phase or phase of the empty nest. The syndrome is a specific cluster of symptoms, including low energy, depression, and sleep problems. These symptoms are caused by one main factor: the emptiness of your home. This emotional disturbance causes many parents to feel anxious about their future goals, especially their ability to attract new partners.

Many women experiencing this syndrome show symptoms like, but not limited to, the following:
- Changes in appetite, weight loss or gain,
- Low energy, fatigue, and a loss of interest in activities,
- Trouble sleeping and trouble concentrating
- Feelings of depression and irritability, especially with their spouse or partner over the messy house.
- Negative thoughts and feelings, including a sense of hopelessness and helplessness.
- Changes in sexual desire, including an unexplained decrease in the frequency of sex.

When you are left with only one child, you are in a state of emotional chaos. You may feel worried about the future of your relationship, your ability to find a mate, and the household's financial well-being. These feelings of anxiety bring on mood swings and even a lack of motivation and feeling overworked.

The Empty Nest Syndrome can be difficult for some parents, especially when dealing with other personal issues such as divorce or depression. Feeling lonely is something that most people try to avoid, but there are many things that you can do to overcome these feelings and start finding happiness again.

The main difference between this syndrome and postpartum depression is that postpartum depression usually lasts a few months after childbirth and also includes feelings of guilt towards your baby for leaving them. However, not all women with this syndrome will experience all symptoms. Most parents are accustomed to spending most of their time with their children. After the children leave home, parents may feel lonely, unsupported, or unsure about what to do with their free time. However, this doesn't mean that parents aren't also experiencing feelings of sadness, loneliness, and a sense of failure. In fact, it is estimated that as many as 40 million mothers and fathers in the United States experience Empty Nest Syndrome. Emotional symptoms of the syndrome may be accompanied by physical symptoms such as fatigue, irritability, and insomnia. Most parents describe the Empty Nest Syndrome as a period of extreme stress. As their child or children leave home and prepare to establish their own lives, parents may feel anxious about their own future. Although most parents enjoy this new freedom, they must also adjust to the loss of regular contact with their children. They worry that they will become easily bored without children in the house, especially when they are used to being around young ones constantly. Parents may also experience feelings of personal failure when they realize that there is nothing to fill up their new-found time and energy with.

To cope with the Empty Nest Syndrome, most parents try to fill their days by going back to work or doing activities they enjoyed before they had children. This can be a difficult transition because they are used to spending all their time with their children. However, many new parents try very hard to deal with these feelings and make themselves feel better. Some mothers begin making changes in their lives, such as joining a book club or joining a recreational sports team. These activities can be useful in helping them deal with their feelings and coping mechanisms for the Empty Nest Syndrome. As parents adjust to the Empty Nest Syndrome, they must also deal with the feelings that it brings up. Some parents feel tremendous guilt over leaving their children alone. They feel especially guilty when they experience feelings of envy toward their peers who still have children at home. Others may become depressed about their lack of a partner, and some mothers may become severely depressed because of these feelings. Other mothers describe this phase as almost "empty," unable to find any meaning in life without a child or children.

The feeling of emptiness is not easy to deal with, and it will take time for most people to recover from it. However, the Empty Nest Syndrome is a temporary condition that can be overcome. The symptoms of the syndrome will begin to ease and return to normalcy once your child leaves home. If you are experiencing feelings of depression and anxiety, these feelings may continue to persist if you are not able to find new activities that will help you cope. You must begin looking for new friends, taking an interest in your hobbies, and attempting new things.

- **Mothers are more at risk.**

The Empty Nest Syndrome mainly affects mothers, but fathers may also experience it. The Empty Nest Syndrome is more likely to occur in women than men, especially in the first few years after the children leave home. Around six out of ten moms who are experiencing Empty Nest Syndrome report high levels of anxiety, depression, and loneliness. The Empty Nest Syndrome is also more common in couples who have a history of marital distress, particularly if they have experienced marital conflict and separation. The Empty Nest Syndrome appears not to affect men as much as it affects women. This is because men are less likely to express or discuss their feelings. Women are very emotional and express the impacts of the Empty Nest Syndrome openly.

Even though Empty Nest Syndrome is common, it's not compulsory that everyone must experience it. Many parents are pleased with the new circumstances life has given them. They enjoy the freedom of no longer having children at home and feel confident that they have prepared their kids well for independent living. Some moms in an empty nest stage feel a sense of relief, especially if their kids are grown and out of the house or out on their own. Women who develop roles that coincide with a declining motherly role experience less stress whether their children depart or not.

Why is the Empty Nest Syndrome common in women?

According to a report by the American Psychological Association (APA) in 2005, "Research suggests that childrearing has a direct impact on women's emotions, both at work and at home. This is because there are gender differences in terms of how women understand their roles as mothers and spouses". In fact, according to the APA report, if single mothers spend too much time tending to their children, they may not receive adequate help from their partners. In addition, both men and women tend to objectify themselves when they assume a caregiving role. When it comes to being perceived as a good mother, Research suggests that women are held more accountable for their performance than men. If women tend to idealize themselves as mothers, this may have an impact on the Empty Nest Syndrome.

Research has shown that differences in gender norms affect how men and women cope with the Empty Nest Syndrome. For instance, some studies indicate that fathers who leave their wives may experience greater guilt than other men. Researchers believe that this is because the departure of their wives disrupts the traditional masculine role of providing for the family. In addition, some research suggests that men who are more committed to their work are less aware of being a parent at home.

In addition to gender issues, other possible contributing factors may affect your experience of this syndrome as you age out.

The Empty Nest Syndrome is not an inevitable stage of life that you cannot avoid. It is a natural reaction to the changes taking place in your life as your children leave home and become independent. You may feel grief because you have lost something special in your life and anxiety about what the future has in store for you.

- **Will you absolutely have this syndrome?**

No. Many people do not experience the Empty Nest Syndrome, or they experience it to a minimal extent. In fact, less than half of the parents who experience an empty nest exhibit symptoms that are greater than those of non-empty nesters. Remember that your children leaving home is not a reflection of your parenting or how much you love them. It does not mean you must be depressed or anxious about life after your children leave home. You should never think this way because it will only worsen the situation.

Although you may not have felt depressed throughout your entire childhood and as an adult, when children leave home, it is normal to feel both sad and anxious about missed opportunities. Whether or not children departed, you will always look back at each stage of your life and experience the sadness of what you missed. You will be sad because you lost something special in your life and anxious about the future because you are unsure how life will unfold. The Empty Nest Syndrome is commonly thought to be a common experience that every parent goes through. However, this is not completely true. Some people simply have no idea that there is a syndrome like the Empty Nest Syndrome or even a name for it. These people feel anxiety and depression but are not aware of it as an actual disorder; because it does not affect the individual's everyday functioning, it is often overlooked. The Empty Nest Syndrome does not mean that you did something wrong during your children's upbringing but think before interfering with your child's life, so they don't leave you behind when they do leave home.

A possible solution to the Empty Nest Syndrome is to make a conscious effort to engage in activities that you enjoy. Take time for yourself, educate yourself, and become a better individual. Learning new skills can help overcome loneliness and provide a sense of purpose. Maybe it's time to learn a new skill and do something you have always wanted to do but put off because of the worries about how you will spend your free time. You may want to go back to school and obtain further education or look into a new career path. Many individuals have found that having children has helped them grow as people and transition from one stage in life to another. You can take advantage of what you learned as a child about building relationships with others and developing your own unique potential.

Even though Empty Nest Syndrome is common, it's not compulsory that everyone must experience it. Many parents are pleased with the new circumstances life has given them.

• How long will it last?

The empty nest stage can last a few years. It will not last forever and can be a positive part of your life. However, some couples may need time to adjust to this change, especially if they do not have the time alone they desire. This stage should not be feared but rather recognized as an opportunity to grow in many ways. An empty nest can be a difficult time for parents. It is common to experience many feelings, such as loneliness, sadness, and depression. Parents might be concerned about their ability to find new ways to fill their time after the children leave home.

Post-Empty Nest Syndrome is the feeling parents are left with once their children leave home, and they start to realize how lonely they feel without them around. Some parents experience this feeling when they see other people who are still in the middle of raising their kids or when they realize that as much as they love their kids, it is not easy work taking care of them all the time. An anticipatory emotional response is a sadness and depression that a parent might experience when they know their child is growing up and his or her childhood is going to end. This may cause parents to prevent themselves from engaging in activities that might remind them of their child and may cause them to isolate themselves.

The following factors determine how long the syndrome will last:

1. How do you feel about your child going away to college and the amount of contact you have with your child?

2. How much independence you provide your children during their teen years and how close they are to you when it comes time for them to leave home.

3. Whether or not you were able to get a job after the kids left home, which will help you meet new people and engage in new activities.

4. Whether or not your spouse has a job that is separate from yours, so if your spouse is working, he or she can provide some structure for activities outside of the house (like date nights and sports events).

5. Whether or not you have a hobby such as gardening, knitting, or reading that keeps you busy and engaged in your life. If not, this may cause some anxiety or depression over the months until your child returns home again from college.

6. How much time do you have to feel lonely if your children are still around (which is not always a bad thing)?

7. The amount of faith you have that they will return to visit and how much you value and enjoy the company of people outside your family (friends, coworkers, and community leaders).

8. Whether or not you have a support system in place to help you cope in your new life when the nest is empty (having a therapist and/or life coach, a network of friends and family, and/or faith leaders).

9. The strength of your relationship with your spouse and the importance of spending time alone together.

10. The amount of time since your last child left home (it could be years, or it could be only a few months).

- **How to cope**

It is essential to find a way to cope with the Empty Nest Syndrome. There are many different ways people cope with it; some parents choose to focus on their future and take advantage of the free time they have. Others do not feel the need to spend a lot of time alone or with themselves. For example, some parents may begin a new hobby, such as gardening or cooking for others in their new family. Some parents find their spouse a separate job so they can engage in new activities without feeling guilty about it.

Many mature couples decide to avoid any activities that remind them of their child and set aside time alone together during this transitional period.

Couples can adjust their schedule to accommodate the changes that children make. As their children leave home, many couples decide to spend less time together and schedule date nights at least two or three times per week, if not more. Couples often work out schedules together so they can see each other on weekends, even if they are spending these days alone.

Some couples also choose to spend time with family members or friends who are still raising their own children so they do not feel lonely and isolated; this is something your child will appreciate. A few like living in a group home and being around other people. Other people choose to live on the beach or near the mountains, where they can enjoy the outdoors, or even in their own homes to get away from it all. Some couples work out their relationship at this point so that their children will know how to handle their future relationships and also provide them with proper examples of what to do. Some people feel lonely and are not sure where to turn with that feeling, but all you really have is yourself and your relationship with your spouse. It is important not to be alone when you're feeling this way. It is okay to seek out your friends and family, or even a therapist or life coach, to help you deal with it.

Even though this journey is difficult at times, you will be able to enjoy the other benefits of being an empty nester. These couples can look forward to spending more time traveling, having fun, and relaxing.

This stage in life can be both enjoyable and stressful for the parents; however, it can also be very rewarding. Many people decide to take their time and make the best of it. This way, they will not regret any aspect of their lives if they do not feel like anything was wasted when their children were young.

The Empty Nest Syndrome is not only experienced when a child goes off to college but also when a child marries and leaves home, even if they do not go far.

This feeling seems to be more common in women than in men. Women often work outside of the home, and they experience this more often than men, who may not want to leave their wives alone with the kids for too long.

The next chapter will focus on how you may be feeling right now and the difficulties you are facing or may face in this important transition in your life.

Chapter Two

Consequences of the Empty Nest Syndrome

Prevalent depressive symptoms in empty nesters are estimated at 46.5%, but in women, it rises to 50%.

The consequences of the Empty Nest Syndrome include:

1. **Loneliness**: Many parents start to feel lonely when their children leave the house. The Empty Nest Syndrome can bring about loneliness for some parents. Loneliness entails the feeling of being alone, the feeling that no one understands you, or the feeling that there is no one to talk to. It is common for a feeling of loneliness to lead to depression in some adults. Loneliness makes the parent feel more vulnerable. They worry about the future and their quest for purpose and meaning and often get sad. Nostalgia, especially for childhood events, can overwhelm the adult. Sometimes, the

empty nest experience tends to make one feel a bit dejected and disappointed.

2. **Disorientation**: A sense of disorientation might be experienced by a parent who has not been prepared for this stage, is already experiencing other life stressors, or simply does not know how to deal with their children no longer being dependent. You lose purpose in life when your kids leave, and you begin to wonder why you picked up the house or cooked dinner every day. Your identity is gone, too. You may feel like you are no longer a parent. Some people describe this feeling as a feeling of emptiness or falling into a void. Your sense of purpose and identity can be restored when you re-assess your life's meaning and then make a change to better it. The Empty Nest Syndrome comes with a lot of stress that has an effect on how people perceive and react to everyday situations. This is because they have to deal with more time on their hands to think about things and events which they could not confront before children occupied their lives. At the same time, people in this situation are less efficient at problem-solving, so they can become easily irritated by the smallest change.

3. **Frustration**: For years, a parent has been used to scheduling the children's activities (such as soccer practice, ballet lessons, art classes, swim team, etc.) and making decisions for the children regarding their education and health. With the absence of children, a parent may feel frustrated. Frustration is characterized by a sense of losing control over the children's activities and being left out of their decision-making. You may want to be in control of your

children but realize that you really don't have any say in what they do or how they behave. With your child being away, you don't get to know about their day like you used to. This may cause a parent to feel anger.

4. **Painful Emotions:** If a parent experiences a painful emotion, such as loneliness, frustration, anger, or frustration and anger, he or she might experience pain in his mind and body. This is called psychosomatic pain. Psychosomatic pain is the kind of physical pain that people feel in their bodies because of emotional discomfort. Psychosomatic pain includes depression and anxiety (behaviors that result from difficult emotions). The ability to grasp one's own emotions is another way in which feelings become expressed in something "physical."

A parent's or especially mother's guilt is one of the most common feelings that people have when their kids move out of the house. They feel guilty for wanting to do things for themselves and for being old enough to raise children, but they are no longer doing so. Parents might even feel guilty about spending time in the company of their friends as this is time also taken away from their children. The good thing is that the parent's guilt usually diminishes within the first year after leaving the nest. However, for some mothers, the guilt lasts for 15 years or longer.

5. **Difficulties with your partner:** When raising kids, many parents pay full attention to their children and neglect the marriage. When the kids leave, parents might realize how distanced they feel from each other, or they may start noticing their rela-

tionship's negative aspects. You may not know what to do with yourselves as a couple. The Empty Nest Syndrome will call your partner's attention to some things you may have ignored or not addressed in the past. It is important to understand that while this adjustment time can be difficult, it can also be a time of growth and renewal for both people. This stage can bring about relationship challenges, but it is a stage you must go through.

6. **Worrying and anxiety**: A parent might become more anxious and worried about their children during this stage. Parents worry about their children's safety, security, health, and well-being. Some parents worry that they are to blame for something bad happening to their children. A parent may lack confidence in the children's ability to be on their own. Parents might start to worry about their own issues; this may be a difficult time for them. They might be worried about their job, finances, or hobbies. They might feel like they have nowhere to turn, and if they are not ready, they may feel very sad and lonely.

Gender is the single factor that can lead to Empty Nest Syndrome. Women with a male partner are less likely to feel alone because of the masculine presence in their home. Men tend to feel lonely, leaving them more susceptible to depression and anxiety. These feelings may become even more intense if their partners leave or divorce.

7. **Depression**: Some parents experience depression along with this stage. For example, a parent who was highly stressed and depressed at the time their children left home will feel depressed

by the emptiness they feel by their children's absence. They may experience more stress, reduce sleep and have new anxieties, such as worries about their financial stability. Some parents might find it difficult to become involved in social activities or hobbies that used to be important to them before their children left home. A parent might even feel like medication can improve things when this is not the case for everyone. Learning to love your child from a distance comes with a lot of grief, fear, and problems. A parent needs to talk about these emotions with a professional without judgment or shame because it is not something one goes through alone.

Sometimes, depression leads to alcohol or drug abuse by parents. The emptiness of home can make one want to medicate it away best as they can. They can only imagine what life outside the home might be like in a positive way. If positive memories about family life are dominated by memories of sibling fighting and other stressful factors, it is not surprising that leaving the nest is so difficult. Feelings of depression and anxiety may persist even after moving out of the nest if still living with parents or siblings so accustomed to them in their younger years.

8. **Identity crisis**: Having children is a significant part of many adults' lives. The identity crises that some parents go through can lead to deep depression and even thoughts of suicide. Some parents are so unhappy with their lives that they cannot take care of themselves. They may decide to give up on life, throw in the towel, break up with their partner or become a recluse. In some cases, these identity crises result in a parent having thoughts about their

child's death. People who have lost their child are at a higher risk for developing suicidal ideation, and this is when it becomes harder for them to live as well as it used to be before the loss of their child or children. Statistically, the rate of depression has been increasing in the past decade. Approximately 20% of adults have experienced depression in their lifetimes. About 2% of adults experience severe depression at any given time. In adolescents, it is not uncommon to see depressive symptoms whenever they are separated from their parents or siblings, and they often feel that this transition from one role to the next (adolescence) can be very difficult for them too. While some kids may feel comforted by their peers, depressed children are more prone to withdraw from friends and activities, making them feel more isolated. Parents should always ensure that these feelings of isolation cannot be suffocated under a misperception about being a burden on others.

Empty Nest Syndrome quiz. Answer with 1 being I strongly disagree and 5 being I strongly Agree

Community

1. Giving back is important to you, and you have scheduled time for a specific cause. 1-2-3-4-5

2. You spend more time talking about your kids when out with your friends. 1-2-3-4-5

3. You are a social person with many friends, but their social media posts make you feel like you aren't that close or connected. 1-2-3-4-5

4. You've always been the "pretty girl," but when you go out with your friends, you don't get all the attention you expect. This makes you feel invisible. 1-2-3-4-5

Identity

5. You often feel inferior to highly accomplished working women in social situations. 1-2-3-4-5

6. You consider your best friend to be more beautiful and accomplished than you, but you aren't jealous. You're just glad that you're on the same team. 1-2-3-4-5

7. You see a post about someone's grief on their child going off to college. You have the same feelings. 1-2-3-4-5

Relationship

8. You see your partner's phone on the counter with neutral texts coming from a person, not in his usual contacts. Do you decide to check? 1-2-3-4-5

9. Your husband spends his weekends doing his own thing, golfing, cycling and you have decided you will take it up also so you can spend some quality time with him. 1-2-3-4-5

10. When just the two of you are out for dinner, you find that both of you are on your phones. You have become one of the couples that doesn't talk to each other. 1-2-3-4-5

Add up your scores.

Community, possible score 4-20. Community is feeling connected to a group of people around us. Having a separate group of people who are going thru the same changes as us. Building a community is a great step in adding value and making a difference in our lives.

Identity, possible score 3-15. Identity is having a sense of who you are inside, separate from your children. Knowing yourself is an important step in being able to increase the confidence that you will be ok.

Relationship, possible score 3-15. Relationship is understanding where you are with your partner so you can continue to build your future.

The next chapter will help you understand why you are where you are today. While reading it, be true to yourself in recognizing which of these factors are true to you. This will help you through the successful implementation of the healing plan offered.

Chapter Three

Risk factors

"**M**othering takes up all the space in your head. When my sons left for school, I cried and cried, and entered a depression. It's really a form of grieving."- Sabina Brennan

Empty Nest Syndrome is a hot topic among adults of divorced parents. When a parent divorces, many challenges can occur post-divorce. Many of which are directly related to the parent that left home. The risk factors include:

1. Unemployed mothers: The Empty Nest Syndrome affects unemployed mothers significantly. The risk factor is mainly attributed to the lack of economic resources that causes a lack of fulfillment in daily life. They also worry about their ability to raise a family and how others perceive them. Mothers who are unable to fulfill all the expectations of their roles in life are often said to be experiencing the Empty Nest Syndrome. The risk factor is primarily attributed to a lack of confidence and low self-esteem, which causes them not to feel fulfilled. There is also a lack of benefits from relationships with others and many other resources that can be obtained from others.

2. **Single mothers:** Single mothers can experience Empty Nest Syndrome when the children leave home. These single mothers live on one income and may be experiencing divorce. Single mothers are at risk of using the internet to deal with their feelings and have higher stress levels regarding their finances. They can search the internet for information about how to budget their money and find ways to cope with the Empty Nest Syndrome by getting used to it. The internet is a good source of information that is easy to access and also free of cost. Single mothers can learn a lot from the internet, such as tips on how to use time effectively and use effective tools or measures that will help them deal with their new situation more easily.

3. **Medical factors:** It is well known that Empty Nest Syndrome can also be related to medical problems. When a person suffers from depression, it often affects their ability to perform tasks that used to be easy for them. A thriving professional life can also be negatively affected by Empty Nest Syndrome. It is considered a risk factor in women with medically established depression and other mental and physical diseases in women diagnosed with postpartum depression. Research shows that women with postpartum depression develop a negative outlook on the world and may have their symptoms worsen during the period when their children leave home.

4. Isolation and loneliness: It is common for women to feel isolated and lonely, especially if they are living in a small town. Loneliness can be a risk factor that impacts their feelings of isolation and depression. The risk factor of loneliness is closely associated with the lack of social life, which can affect the way in which they cope with the Empty Nest Syndrome. The lack of contact with others can affect their mental health because the people around them can no longer provide them with what they need.

5. Stay-at-home mom: This is a risk factor that describes a mother who decides to stay at home with the children. It is the only scenario where both parents will have time for them. The Empty Nest Syndrome can cause anxiety and depression among these mothers. They may feel out of place because they feel like they are being left behind. They are used to having their children around, so they see it as a loss when they leave home.

6. Difficulty dealing with change: Most of the families that they have left will not be the same as the ones they had when they left. The family may include children that are still in school and others who have gotten married and divorced during their absence. They may also find it hard to adjust to being without their parents, even if they still live in the same neighborhood. The Empty Nest Syndrome can cause a feeling of loss, helplessness, and depression. They may feel like they will never be the same again because they have lost the only constant in their life.

7. Difficulty with your own moving out of home: The Empty Nest Syndrome can make the transition to the new house or apartment difficult. People who are experiencing Empty Nest Syndrome are vulnerable to experiencing loneliness and often seek help from family support groups, as well as professional counseling for things such as depression when dealing with change. Leaving home can be a big change that they could never have prepared for. They may worry about their ability to cope with their own parents and children leaving home. They feel that they will never be able to live alone again and that they won't be capable of coping with all the responsibilities of being an independent adult.

8. Not trusting your child on their own: This risk factor can lead to children who can no longer be independent. Parents with Empty Nest Syndrome tend to worry about their children and often use the internet as a way to deal with their feelings. They want to give them all the resources they need, but they are worried that they won't be able to take care of themselves. Parents with Empty Nest Syndrome can feel guilty about not being there to provide their guidance and help them out in their time of need.

9. Other losses such as retirement or menopause: These losses can also lead to Empty Nest Syndrome or a feeling of loss because they can no longer do the things they used to do before. These people may have retired and have lost their social circle. Some of them may have experienced loneliness and the inability to regularly spend time with their peers, which can cause depression. Menopause causes a loss of estrogen, making it difficult for them to deal with the changes in their bodies. Depression is often associated with Empty Nest Syndrome in these types of situations.

The Empty Nest Syndrome can also be triggered by some other losses, such as retirement or menopause, that lead women who are experiencing it to feel like they will never be the same again because they have lost the only constant in their life.

10. Unmet expectations: Women who don't think that they have an active role in the family while they are at home with their children may feel disappointed if they have used up their energy helping out with the housework or raising the kids and no one asks them for help when it comes time to prepare for the Empty Nest Syndrome. This can make them feel like their expectations were not met.

11. Your parenting style: There are two types of parenting styles.

• *Helicopter parent:* This refers to a parent who hovers over their children and tends to do everything for them. They have difficulty letting go because they think their children cannot cope without them.

• *Stay-at-home parent:* This refers to a parent who has decided to take responsibility for the entire household and all the chores that it requires. They are aware of their children being independent but unwilling to relax because they feel their children aren't mature enough.

These parents may experience Empty Nest Syndrome because they can no longer spend time only with their children. They may also feel like they will never be the same again because they have lost the only constant in their life.

12. You have low income: Women who have low-income levels tend to have Empty Nest Syndrome because they have a less active role in the household. They may feel like they can no longer help out with the children, and it causes them to experience loneliness because they often don't have friends who can provide companionship.

13. You do not take good care of yourself: Women who don't take good care of themselves often experience Empty Nest Syndrome because they don't feel they can do everything they want. They see it as a time for them to enjoy life, but instead, they feel depressed about the fact that their children have grown up and left home.

14. You do not have friends when your child leaves: Women who do not have friends when they leave home usually experience experiences of Empty Nest Syndrome because they see it as a time for them to relax and rest, but instead, they are left alone. They don't have anyone to take care of them at home or enjoy their company as much as they used to before.

15. How well you built your family skills: If a woman does not have good family skills, she may experience Empty Nest Syndrome because she does not feel that she is able to cope with her own kids leaving. She may also feel that it is a time for them to get away and enjoy themselves, but they instead find themselves depressed and lonely because they no longer have their children around.

Things may seem very difficult right now. You may even feel stuck in those hard feelings you are experiencing right now. But remember, change is a part of life. The next chapter will help you understand the natural progress of Empty Nest Syndrome.

Chapter Four

Stages of Empty Nest Syndrome

"I remember counting the days to each holiday or whenever I would get to see my son again."- Rachel Baer

A parent may have mixed emotions about their child leaving. As a child leaves home, the parent may feel heartbreak for the first time because they have lost them. They may also be excited for their child to go off and do new things, but it can also be difficult for them to feel like they are no longer needed. This can lead to stress and anxiety because they don't know how to deal with their feelings of loss. These tend to be the stages that parents will experience when they go through Empty Nest Syndrome:

- **Stage 1. Grief**

Feelings of sadness and loss when your child leaves. This stage can start out very gradually and is often a combination of many different emotions. Those who are experiencing fear may have to deal with feelings of panic, sadness, loneliness, and possibly even anger. Denial and self-pity also compound grief.

Denial in the sense that some parents will not want to recognize that their child is growing up. They will want to believe that they still need to take care of them and help them with everything they are going through in life. This can make it hard for them to accept that their child has grown up.

Self-pity results from the realization that you will be alone and no longer have the time to just do things for yourself because you are taking care of the house. You have put all your energy into raising the kid you have invested so much in, and it sometimes makes it difficult for you to accept that they will never need you again.

Self-pity can also result when parents worry about how they are going to fill up their time after their child leaves home. Will they be able to take care of themselves? Will they feel lonely?

Symptoms of the grief stage

Grieving parents often feel extremely guilty about the fact that they are grieving. They may ask themselves, "Why can't I just be happy for my child? Why do I keep crying?" This shows up as feelings of being deprived, sulky, and lazy.

Some bereaved parents are so wrapped up in themselves and their feelings that they don't notice their child growing up. They will want to keep the child as a little boy or girl even when they are a teenager. They will want to call them over for dinner every night and expect that everything will be the same. This may make them feel guilty because it is adult behavior, and they are being selfish by not enjoying the new relationship between both parties. Parents may feel guilty about other things they have done to their children while growing up. Even if they didn't do anything to them, they might feel guilty that they didn't do enough. They might even tell themselves that it was their fault for not knowing how to be a parent. If a parent spends too much time thinking about what he or she hasn't done as a parent, this will lead to negative thoughts, which can affect the grieving process. You need to remember all the good things you have done as a parent and try your best not to think about all your mistakes.

Here are some other symptoms of the grief stage:

1. Anger: Some parents will be angry with their children for leaving. This can result from how they have raised their child, or just because they want to be angry that they cannot keep control over them, or because they feel their needs are not being met and wish to punish them. This can also result from the fear that when their child leaves home, he or she will not come back. They feel angry because they enjoy having a family, and now that their child is leaving, the family might break up.

2. Fear: Fear is an emotion that often arises when a child leaves home to go to college or live on his or her own. Parents may fear that their child will not be able to survive on his or her own in the outside world. They are afraid of what life will be like after they leave and also afraid they may never be able to see them again. It is scary to be on your own, and it may make you feel vulnerable because you have no one to depend on. Parents also fear their children will not follow the same morals that they have instilled in them. They fear their child will no longer care about them or think about what is best for him or her.

They may also fear certain situations, such as if their child will be able to handle being able to balance a full-time job and social life, how they are going to pay for college, and anything else that comes up along the way.

If parents have successfully raised their child up until this point, they might fear that now that their kid is gone, they won't be able to take care of themselves. They may feel lonely, scared, and upset that they have lost control over their child. They might also fear that losing their child will affect them too much, and they may be left feeling like they can't go on. Sometimes parents don't want to be alone because they are afraid it will make them feel depressed or won't give them the energy to do anything with themselves.

3. Sadness and worry: Sadness is a normal emotion that comes with the grief stage. This is often the most difficult, but it should not last forever. Parents should know that sadness should last at least a couple of weeks. It will pass, and they will eventually move on to another stage called acceptance/recovery, or the relief stage.

They may feel sorrowful because they think about when their kids were small. They are sad because their children are growing up and will no longer be dependent on them for everything to be okay in life. They can also feel worried because now that their child has left home, they may not be able to make them happy anymore. If a parent feels worried because they are unsure how they will take care of themselves, this will affect the grieving process.

4. Externalizing and isolation: Externalizing is when a person re-directs his or her anger outward. They find something else to be mad at to avoid being angry with themselves. Sometimes parents might be angry at their children for not accepting the fact that they need to move out. They might see it as an act of betrayal or see their kids as brats for not wanting to leave home. Some parents may also externalize their anger towards anyone or anything else in their family who disagrees with them about the situation. This will affect the grieving process because it will cause the parent to feel even angrier.

Externalizing is a defense mechanism against accepting responsibilities. This can lead to them feeling like they have to be in control of everything and make sure that everything goes their way. Their child's life is also no longer under their control, which upsets them, so they try to regain control by being mad at anyone who doesn't agree with them being upset. If parents choose to externalize their anger, then these emotions should come out healthily. For example, they can get together with a couple of friends, talk about how they are feeling, and try to work through the situation together. Or they can go to counseling.

5. Denial: A parent may feel like their child is still young and will return home after their first year of college, or even if their child is a teenager, they may think that he or she will return home after only one or two years. These feelings can be resolved when a parent has accepted the situation for what it is, but this may take some time before it happens. If a parent doesn't accept the reality of what has happened in their lives, then this will affect the grieving process.

6. Regret: Regret is another feeling that a parent may feel. Sometimes they will feel regret that they have raised their children and now have to face the consequences of habits they have developed over time. They might blame themselves for not having as much time to spend with family as they used to.

These are just some of the different emotions that parents may experience when a child leaves home for the first time or when any other major event occurs in their lives, such as losing a job or someone close to them passing away. Emotions are very important in life, but sometimes it's better not to dwell on feelings if they can affect your physical and mental health or cause you to become depressed.

- **Stage 2. Relief**

This is the second stage in the process of Empty Nest Syndrome. It is a time for parents to begin to feel free and enjoy their freedom. They may experience happiness, excitement, and also guilt. They may feel a sense of calmness and peace because they no longer rely on themselves for everything. Parents will learn a lot about themselves during this stage. They will learn more about who they are as people and what they want out of life now that they no longer have children. Parents learn to accept themselves and their feelings and learn how to live life on their own. This is when they start to accept the fact that they will not be able to fix things for themselves now that their children have left home.

During this time, parents will come up with new plans for their life, such as going back to school or finding a new career path that you can start from scratch again. This stage can be very positive because it is when some parents realize that they have time to themselves, and they can have a good night's sleep and do everything they have been yearning to do.

Symptoms of the relief stage

At this stage, many parents have learned to accept that their children have grown and realized these benefits. They no longer need to do everything for their kids and can accept that they have lives of their own. They start to live independently and make decisions without worrying about the consequences. This is a good time for them because they have the freedom to do what they want, but it can also be difficult because parents still have some feelings of emptiness inside. At this stage, a parent may experience the following:

1. A spirit of adventure: This is when a parent begins to explore the world on their own. They may travel a lot, take classes, or try new things. They may want to start a hobby or learn something new.

2. Freedom from responsibility: When children leave home, parents no longer have to worry about them and begin to feel more relaxed and less stressed out. Stress levels are usually lower in parents because they no longer have their kids around them all the time and can do whatever they want without worrying about their child being upset with them for not doing what they wanted them to do at that particular time.

3. A sense of relief: Parents feel relieved because they no longer have the responsibility of taking care of their children. When they are free from this, they can do more things that they want to do. They may want to clean up their surroundings more and make changes in their homes that they have long put off doing. They may start to make new plans for their future and start to live life again.

4. Sudden freedom from constriction: People feel free to do things they have always wanted to do but have not been able to do because of their children. They begin to enjoy new hobbies and interests without having a child around them.

5. Feeling energized: Parents feel they can do anything they want, and nothing stops them from doing this. They are able to make changes in their lives that have been put off for a long time and start to enjoy their free time more. Their children may come back one day, but their life will never be the same again since they have grown up independently and made new relationships during this stage.

6. A sense of accomplishment: Parents will feel a sense of accomplishment and satisfaction when their kids finally learn to take care of themselves. They may see that their children have grown up and can care for themselves independently. After all, they have given them a lot, and they can now see the fruits of their labor.

Parents will feel great for having given their children enough attention and love when they were kids. They can see that being a parent is not just ensuring that your child eats, goes to school, and does his or her homework all the time. There's more to it than that; parents can see the changes their children have gone through as adults because of their experiences when they left home.

7. A feeling of being liberated: Parents may feel confident and comfortable on their own for the first time. They no longer have to take care of their children and can do whatever they want to do. Parents will have more energy because they no longer have to worry about taking care of their kids. This is a great time for adults because they are able to start over again, make a new life, and live life on their own without worrying about the kids and how they will react when they return home one day.

- ## Stage 3. Joy and freedom

This is the third stage in Empty Nest Syndrome because now that the child has left, you can finally relax. You no longer have to worry about taking care of their household or keeping up with their schedule. You are not putting yourself through so much stress because you know that they are getting on with their lives and won't need you anymore. You can focus on your own life instead of worrying about what they are doing. You may also be feeling guilty that you were able to relax while they were still living at home because it is now your time to enjoy life without any responsibilities. It is a time for parents to start making new plans for themselves and start over again from scratch.

Symptoms of the joy stage

The joyfulness stage occurs because the Empty Nest Syndrome is ending, and parents can finally relax. You no longer have to worry about your children since they can now live their own lives. You can start over again and do whatever you want without any restrictions. This is a great time for you because you can catch up on things that were on hold due to all your responsibilities as a parent. You feel confident that you can start over again, get a fresh new start, and live life on your own without fearing what your children will do without you in the future.

1. You are relieved because: At this point, you are no longer stressed out about what your children are doing, but you may be worrying about how they will adapt to their new environment. In the past, you were always worried about how they would react when they finally left home and started their own families. Now that they have left, you can take a break and think about your own life and what you want to do in the future without having to worry about them or the things that they need from you for them not to be upset with you in the future.

2. You are easygoing: You can finally relax and enjoy your life no matter what you do in the future. You can do things you have always wanted to do long ago but never had the chance to because of your children. This is a great time for you because now that your kids are gone, you feel free from responsibility and can finally live life in whatever way you want.

3. You feel stress-free: With the children out of the house, parents experience less stress than before when their children were still living at home. This is great for parents because they no longer have to worry about their children and the things that they are doing or how they are going to react when they return home one day.

4. You feel energized: Parents feel they can do anything they want, and nothing stops them from doing this. They are able to make changes in their lives that have been put off for a long time and start to enjoy their free time more if they so choose. Their children may come back one day, but their life will never be the same again since there was a change after they grew up and started on their own.

5. You feel happy: You can be yourself and no longer have to worry about what your children are doing. This is when you can finally enjoy your life on your own without having to think about what the child will do for you once they come back home one day. You will feel free and liberated because you have never been so relaxed before in your life.

6. You feel a sense of independence: The Empty Nest Syndrome is ending, and parents can finally do what they want without worrying about their children. They no longer have to think about the day their child starts a family and moves away. This is great for parents because they can finally start over again, make new plans, and enjoy life without any restrictions.

They may have enjoyed their time with their kids, but once the children leave home, the Empty Nest Syndrome will set in for some. It may take some time for parents to get used to life without having to worry about taking care of them anymore since there's no one left at home, and it's just you by yourself once again.

Empty Nest Syndrome Quiz:

1. How did you feel when your child first left home?
- Distressed
- Heavy-hearted
- Relieved
- Elated

2. How do you feel now about not having children at home?
- Distressed
- Heavy-hearted
- Relieved
- Elated

• If you answered distressed or heavy-hearted, you are in stage 1, the grief stage. This stage is the hardest, but usually passes quickly.

Moms miss being involved in their childrens lives and wish for things to be as they used to be.

• If you answered relieved, you are in stage two, the relief stage. This stage is a transitional stage on the way to joy. About 20% of moms go straight here.

• If you answered elated, you are in stage three, the joy stage. This stage is a new beginning. It can take some a while to get here, but all will eventually end up here.

3. How is your marriage?

- Not in a relationship

- Getting better

- The same

- Getting worse

• If you answered getting better, you are an upswinger. These couples are ready to be on their own as the children leave home.

• If you answered the same, you are an even keeler. These couples don't change much after the children leave.

• If you answered getting worse, you are a downslider. These couples don't have a lot left after the children leave. The children were all that was holding the marriage together. It takes a lot of work to put these relationships back together

4. I feel I have (choose one of the following)

- Better control over my life

- Less control over my life
- The same control over my life

• If you answered less control, you are stuck. You may need additional help to get past this feeling and gain more control.

• If you answered the same control, you are a survivor. You still may feel somewhat nervous about what comes next, but are willing to push on.

• If you answered better control, you are a thriver. You take charge of things and tend to recover faster.

Now that you see the light at the end of the tunnel, the next chapter will help you see even clearer how what you are going through is a natural phase in the life of every parent, every woman, and every family. You are not alone in this!

Chapter Five

Family Dynamics: The natural Family Cycle

The second year hasn't been as bad as the first, which started around Christmas, her senior year, and her high school graduation. When we dropped her at school, I thought I was going to die. I was devastated, and stopped eating and sleeping; my parents urged my husband to feed me and make me sleep because I looked horrible in the graduation pictures. I cried all the way home.-Melissa

- **The empty nest is a natural phase.**

There is a natural cycle of change for most family units, the empty nest. However, not all empty nest relationships are created equal. Not all families feel comfortable stepping off the roller coaster together. Some families are wired for a predictable progression at this time in their lives, while some find themselves facing decisions and feelings that they have never experienced before. For some, the empty nest feels like a tremendous loss, while it is a relief for others. For some, the empty nest signals independence, while for others, it's a signal of loneliness and aloneness that wasn't really on the radar before. It's important that we recognize that there will be a range of experiences between these polar opposites because in our rush to compare experiences with others, we can find ourselves feeling abandoned or unneeded or, worse yet, like nothing at all has changed.

As the children are closing in on their last year of school before their teenage years, a natural and expected shift occurs with the focus on their educational commitments, new opportunities, and development. Maybe this was an easy transition for your family, where you feel no different than you did before the kids left to go to college. If this is indeed your experience, then I am sure you appreciate that your children were responsible for setting the stage for what comes next for you.

But for families not walking through this same path of change with ease, there can be much uncertainty. There can be a sense of loss, confusion, frustration, and even anger. This is where the family begins to face these changes head-on and work through their feelings together.

Many people want to compare their experiences with those who had children before them. They may feel like they're not equipped for the changes that are about to come, and no one has ever shared stories before because it's difficult to find others who have gone through this process. But don't compare your own emotions with those that came before you without having asked them first if they would prefer to share their story privately or publicly with the world. When we compare our own experiences with what others have to say, it's important that we also consider how they frame their stories. We must recognize that some people will be very open in sharing their feelings, while others might want to share only a few details or not at all. So whether you are telling your story or listening to someone else's, you must remember how they would choose to be framed and shared for this time in their lives.

The empty nest can be a very positive family transition if there is a willingness to look inwardly and outwardly and explore the feelings that come up during this time. If you can do that, you will be in a better position to start moving forward with peace of mind rather than reactive.

Here are some ways that we can help ourselves to see the positive aspect of this transition and to prepare ourselves for what lies ahead:

1. Begin by acknowledging what is going on inside of us. We can talk about it with each other or work through it alone. Whatever we need to do, this is the time to address if there have been any unresolved issues or if any part of us doesn't feel right in relation to our feelings about our children's departure from college and beyond.

2. Remember that it's okay not to know what to do or feel. No one knows what's coming next for us; this is a healthy place to be. Believe that our children have what they need and that we will be okay no matter what happens next in their lives. Consider the possibility that we may not always be aware of what has happened in their lives or how much is really happening for them at this time in their lives, so do whatever you can to keep checking in on them during this time of transition as well as following up with them periodically later when they are settled into their new lives away from home.

3. Get back in touch with our own priorities. Our children may have helped us refocus our priorities, but now it's time for us to re-focus them ourselves. We must find ways to enjoy our lives and treat ourselves well even if we are not getting the same attention from our children as we're accustomed to having from them.

4. Remember that our relationships with our children are a two-way street. We must always stay connected to them and want to ask plenty of questions and check in often. But it's also important that they remember to stay connected with us. Don't wait for them to initiate contact with you when they have moved away and are busy building their own new lives. Make an effort to connect with them often and find out what's going on in their lives, as well as ask yourself what more you could do to create opportunities for connecting with them, even if it requires some extra planning on your part, such as scheduling regular phone-calls or trips back home.

5. Stay mindful that some changes may not be what we expect them to be. If there is no sadness about the empty nest, then we need to acknowledge that this is healthy for us too, and if we feel a sense of loss and disappointment, then it's important that we consider why. We must consider what new possibilities might be around the corner, what our children's departure might mean for us as parents, and how it might affect our relationships with them. We don't want to close any doors by focusing on what we think is missing in our lives after the kids leave home because they may return sooner than expected or in ways we never imagined.

6. It's helpful to find a "who, what, where, and when" chart for our children to follow in their moves once they have left home. It's also helpful for us to keep up with the "what" since we don't know exactly where they are, who is taking care of them and whether their needs are being met. If we don't keep tabs on the other stuff, it can be very frustrating for those left behind who may not know what's happening with our kids.

7. Remember that all transitions take time. It's important to be aware of our own reactions to this change. We must give ourselves the time we need for sadness, confusion, frustration, and anger to dissipate so we can find our way forward.

8. Remember that it's okay to cry, laugh, jump into action and yell at the kids when they phone home during this transition. It doesn't matter if they're successful in keeping in touch or not: We will live through their successes, and we will live through their disappointments, but it's still all a part of this process together,

and we will rise to meet the challenges together no matter what the outcome may be.

9. Finally, keep the long view in mind. Kids may go away for a few years, only to return home for some time during their visits or even live with us forever. Either way, our children come back to family and friends from before and after, and this will be a good thing for everyone when it happens.

"Use it or lose it" might not apply to everything in life, but when it comes to the competitive spirit of your relationship with your children, if you are not careful, you could lose the edge over them...

We all want to succeed in our relationships with our children. Not good at all, but very common, and also very much avoidable if we can find ways to hold on to the competitive edge over them in the important areas of their lives. Some of us have more success than others, and some are already being outshined by our kids, who can't wait to shove us into the "has been" category.

Carefully choose your battles and then compete hard for them no matter what your children throw at you.

- **Understanding your family cycle helps you transition better.**

Children grow up and leave home, allowing a new generation to do the same. When there's no one around to nag them about eating vegetables and talking nicely, many parents are left with an Empty Nest Syndrome when their children leave for college. But just because your children have gone doesn't mean you're alone in this process. When you've left your family home, it's essential to recognize that the rest of the world has changed, and those changes will likely continue with or without you. That's why it's so important for parents to stay connected and change their expectations accordingly.

Here are some things to consider about your own family cycle:

1. The Current Generation

When your children leave, you start a new generation that looks a lot different from what preceded it. You may find yourself introducing a whole new generation of relatives and friends, especially if you don't have any close friends or relatives who were children when maternal grandparents or great-grandparents passed away. You may also find yourself raising your grandchildren, which can be a lot of fun.

2. The Next Generation

Your children's children grow older and leave the nest. This is usually when grandparents have a new generation of kids to get acquainted with—even if you have never met them before! It can be difficult to bring up your grandchildren without the familiar voices and faces you used to know so well, but it is also an opportunity for new friendships to form and life generally to evolve. Your children's children beget children of their own, and so on, like an endless cycle. It can feel like forever until the next generation emerges, but it's always a good time to make new friends and step out into the bigger world.

3. The Outside World

In the end, your children's departure isn't the end of the world because the outside world continues to evolve and change no matter what you do. Keep an eye out for new opportunities and trends that can benefit your family. For example, if you're a member of a local church, keep in mind that something might come along that can benefit you—and your family as well—and it could be just what you need to make life easier. At times like this, you can trust the Lord to help you through your family cycle and the changes that come with it.

4. Your Personal Development

You may develop into a new type of mother—or return to your childhood self—when your children leave, and you're finally alone again. Maybe you'll decide that it is time for some romantic getaways or even a career change. Or maybe you'll want to get involved in political causes or community programs that interest you but weren't possible before because of all the commitments that parenting requires. Whatever direction you take, it's important to remember that personal development is an important part of the family cycle and something worth embracing without reservation!

5. Your Relationship with Your Partner

When your children leave, it's easy to take the focus off of you and your partner. You may find yourself feeling more distant from one another if you are used to being around kids all the time. However, now is a good time to rediscover each other. Make sure that you're spending quality time together, even if there are empty rooms in your house where children once lived. There are plenty of other things to do in your home, from shopping, preparing meals, paying bills, exercising, reading books, and playing board games together. Your relationship with your partner may be rocky after your children leave, but there is no better time for you to find ways to improve it rather than getting upset about the problems you once thought were permanent.

6. Your Relationship with Your Children

Even if you don't want it to happen, some of your children's friends will leave when yours do. The best way for your children and their friends to say goodbye is by taking care of their business so that you can focus on yourself and each other without distraction. Let each family member know that you have no expectations about how long the farewells should last or the time period for them to return. Soon enough, the time will come when your children no longer need to live away from home and can even return with their friends at some point in their lives. But until then, enjoy being a family of two—two parents and two children—without the added responsibility of being a mother or a father.

Understanding your family cycle will help you make better decisions, understand what is happening and why, and help you to feel more in control of your life. It has been said that each one of us has a period in our lives when we are empty nesters, and each phase of the empty nest has its own issues. Reflecting on your empty nest understanding will allow you to recognize what happened during the phase and help you to prepare for the next phase. Moving from one phase of the family cycle to another is a transition, and transitions are always hard. Understanding the transition helps you to prepare for what comes next and to feel more comfortable with your current situation. For example, if you are parenting on your own now, but you have a teenager or child who is still living at home, then you are experiencing the empty nest phase of your family cycle right now. You can prepare for what comes next by planning ahead and finding ways to stay connected and active in your children's lives while they are at home. Finally, using your understanding of the empty nest stage to find ways to share more of yourself with others in a healthy and meaningful way will help you find your purpose in taking on these transitions.

- **Stages of the natural family cycle**

The family cycle begins with two young people pairing up and beginning their life together as an independent family unit. It is important to acknowledge the beginning stage of the cycle because there are things that need to be prepared for and managed during this time. For example, if one or both partners come from dysfunctional families, they will have some issues that need to be addressed as a couple before they can build a healthy relationship with each other. If one or both partners are unemployed, this needs to be addressed before they start their new family and begin building their life together. Sometimes, situations in one or both partners' lives make this time very difficult, such as sexual abuse; drug or alcohol problems; physical disabilities; medical problems; mental illness, or depression. These two individuals bear or adopt children, leading to an expansion of the family unit. Children are blessed with parents who love them unconditionally, but they also bear the scars of their parents' dysfunction, which are borne with them into adulthood. The enlarged family needs to deal with the issues that got them into this situation in the first place and may need to find help to address their problems because parenting is a difficult job, and it is often easier for a parent to run from their problems than face them head-on. When this happens, there are consequences for their children that often play out over time, and these become issues for future generations of families. The end of the family life cycle is also composed of two people since children grow and eventually move out of the home.

Families with more than one child will have overlapping demands for resources since most children will be of different ages. Let us look at the stages in detail:

Stage 1. Forming and Nesting: This stage begins with marriage and continues until the first child is born. The main concern for this stage is managing responsibilities. Responsibilities can be managed in two ways;

• *Independence*: This means taking on your responsibilities, being responsible for yourself, and getting along with your partner.

• *Coupling or marriage:* This means managing your marriage and your responsibilities as a couple and focusing on your relationship with each other.

This stage continues through the end of the first year of marriage for the majority of couples, but for others, it lasts longer. The length of this stage depends on a number of factors, including how well you handle responsibilities during this time and whether or not you have any physical, mental, or emotional disabilities that could interfere with this phase. Some couples find that they are not ready to begin their family life until they have been married for ten years. You enter into parenthood through the birth or adoption of a child/children.

Stage 2. Expanding the family: This stage begins with the birth of your first child and ends with your last child leaving home. It is important to acknowledge the beginning of this stage because things need to be prepared for and managed during this time. For example, if you have never had a job, you must begin working before your first child is born. If your spouse has no job skills, you may need to find ways to get him/her into a training program or begin saving money so that he/she can return to school.

Parenting your babies through adolescence:

Parents often tell their children that things will improve once they reach adolescence. This is not true. Parenting in teens can be much harder than at any other time in your child's life. Parents have to learn how to manage a teenager's mood swings when angry, sad and happy, as well as find ways to help support their child through their ever-changing moods while undergoing this period of change. Parenting during this stage is also very important because your child needs you and wants your support during these times of growth and development that happens during adolescence.

The end of adolescence is the beginning of the great life change that is college; however, it is important to seek help in advance. It is very common for parents to feel overwhelmed by the idea of their child leaving home for college, and many parents become depressed from this time onwards.

Stage 3. Enjoying your independence: Time will come when your children will leave and start their own families. Before you get to enjoy your freedom fully, there are two factors involved;

• ***Launching children who have now become adults:*** These are children who have left home and now wish to live on their own, but they still need to contribute in some way to the family. You may find that these children need a little "help" in achieving this goal. The help they need may be financial or emotional, but it is important to remember that these children also need your support as they leave home.

• ***Retirement and adventure:*** This is the time for many people to enjoy their retirement and move on to new adventures. You no longer provide for the family, so you can do what you like and look forward to starting new adventures.

The end of this stage is a burst of energy as your children go off on their own and start families of their own.

It is good to know that you are not alone in this. But knowing does not make you feel better, does it? Do not worry; I am here for you. In the next chapter, I offer you my bulletproof plan: 'Stretch

DANI LAI MACGREGOR

Your Old Wings Plan' to offer you all the support, help, and tools you need to find purpose, fulfillment, and happiness in the next phase of your life without your children.

Chapter Six

Stretch your old wings plan

"Start by doing what's necessary; then do what's possible, and suddenly you are doing the impossible." – Francis of Assisi

It may seem impossible now that you have overcome this roller-coaster of feelings that are dragging you down. It may seem impossible to find who you are again now as your kids are gone. It may even feel impossible to enjoy your marriage now that you both are not focusing on the kids, or it may seem impossible to overcome the deep loneliness that you are experiencing as a single mother now that the house is empty. All these impossibilities will be diluted, and you will find who you are and enjoy life as a person and as a couple when you follow the 'Stretch Those Wings Plan' this book offers you.

Step 1. Understand what you are going through: You need to go towards self-acknowledgment and accept the feelings that you are going through. Feelings will continue to surface during your married life, so you must be prepared for that. Mastering your feelings is the first step towards managing this roller-coaster of feelings.

Step 2. Accept your family dynamics: This is where you need to accept your marriage and realize that the family dynamics will change with your children leaving home. You will need to adjust and accept this new situation and their new goals from their life outside the family. Each life cycle ends at some point, and no matter how hard it is, it is important to let go of these negative feelings and emotions.

Step 3. It's time to let go: This is a very crucial step towards healing. Your children have now become adults, and you must let them be and rebuild your relationship from a new point. Your motherly role has changed, and you must come out of that position if you want to rebuild your relationship with your child. Accept the new life, and heal from all the feelings that you are going through.

Step 4. Care for your feelings: Empty nesting stirs in you feelings of sadness, making life very hard. You need to let go of these feelings and begin to care for your feelings. The more you care for your feelings, the more you will be able to walk along life's path with a full heart, knowing that the whole world is yours for the taking. You need to manage your feelings, for this is the only way to combat the feelings of sadness that come with empty nesting.

This will help you to fully cope with empty nesting and move on with your life.

Step 5. After grievance comes life: Your life has taken a new form, and you need to embrace that. You and your children know that you will always be there for each other, but this is your time. Take this time to re-explore who you are as a person, make new friends, or renew old friendships. Pursue the career goals you had earlier put off raising the kids. Allow yourself to enjoy the small joys that life brings and ensure to take good care of yourself while at it.

Pay attention to your spouse and make sure you spend time together. You will find that in this time when your children are gone and have left you, a deeper bond of love has been forged. It will be the time for you to reconnect with your spouse and relish the physical beauty of each other's bodies. You will also see that during this time, you and your spouse have grown so much closer together and enjoy new levels of intimacy.

Now, let's start the change. Your children are your world. Well, not anymore! The next chapter will help you reshape your relationship with your now adult independent children so you and they will enjoy it and maintain your strong bonds as a family even if you are no longer under the same roof.

Chapter Seven

Allow your children to become adults

"It is not what you do for your children, but what you have taught them to do for themselves that will make them successful human beings."- Ann Landers

Even though you are used to controlling everything your children do, it is crucial to take a step back and let them gain control of their lives.

- **Treat their departure as an adventure**

Treating this as an adventure will be better for both you and your children. Look at it as a positive change. Your children are going to be going back and forth between being excited about what is coming to being terrified at the thought of leaving. It's important to be supportive and reassure them that once they are settled, it will be fun and they will be successful. Let them know that your home will always be home for them. That gives them the safety net they need to go out into the world. They may have a hard time at first working thru the separation, just like you, but they need your support.

- **Prepare for them to leave**

If you have an idea of when they will be leaving, getting ready for school, or getting married, make sure you are preparing them to be out on their own. Check and make sure they know how to do the little things:Balance a checkbookCook meals for the dayDo their laundryGet along with their neighborsClean the houseGrocery shop

If you do not know until the last minute, don't panic. Offer them the support they need and let them know you are available to answer any questions they have as they go along. Whatever they can't work out on their own, they will ask when they need it.

This may be the hardest thing to deal with but let them go and encourage them to explore the world and give them a chance to discover who they are without you trying to control their every thought and action.

Remember that difficult times will always try to come back around – use this as an opportunity to become better people. In these situations, you can work on your character and make changes within yourself so that you do not have such challenges in the future.

If there's anything you may learn from the situation, it is about yourself, and what aspects of yourself need improvement so that this does not happen again. You can start preparing them now, while they are still young. Tell them to take the time to discover what they love to do, and engage in that activity as much as possible.

It is your responsibility to help them get started in life and not to burden them further. You and your husband will be there to help with the finances, but you need to encourage them to leave the nest. You will be surprised at how fast they grow up and how quickly they will learn on their own. It is recommended that you allow your children to make mistakes when they are young so that they can learn from those mistakes. They do not want a handout when it comes to learning about life; in fact, you should encourage them and let them seek their own answers instead of being there every step of the way. Remember that you are there to guide them and support them, but never to control the direction of their lives. The main thing is that your children succeed on their own and learn from life's mistakes.

- **Enjoy their growth**

It is a fantastic experience to see your children heading out and making achievements in life. Your children's achievements should be the source of your joy because they are the gift of life. The best thing you can do to deal with empty nesting is to encourage them and help them grow with the right advice and input for their lives.

THE EMPTY NEST DISCOVER YOUR NEW LIFE FOCUS

It's time for you to also move on from your position as a "mother" and become a helpful buddy to your adult kids. You need to let go of your feelings of control and embrace the fact that your children are now in charge of their lives. Try to be more patient and understand that this is also a hard time for them as they start growing up and becoming independent adults.

Parents can get very controlling when it comes to their children leaving home. You can be there to guide and support them as they navigate through college, university, relationships, and work, but you have to make sure that you do not get tangled up in their personal lives. You have to let go of your annoyance if you find out that your children have not followed your advice. Things might not be the way that you wanted them, but they could turn out better this way. You must try to keep things positive because it helps ease the struggle of letting your kids fly the nest. You might feel like you are grieving because they are leaving, and you won't be able to see them every day anymore, but there is a big difference between grief and letting go. Grief means you are not ready to let your children go, while letting go means you are ready to enjoy the rest of your lives.

Step back and focus on something else; keep yourself busy. When you stop focusing on what is missing, it becomes easier for you to enjoy the things that you have by yourself. You need to give yourself time for activities that keep away feelings of loneliness. Take a class, join an activity club, or become more involved with the church community because it will keep your mind off the missing kids. You can also use this as an opportunity to reconnect with yourself, your partner, and your relationship.

Don't wait for someone else to step in.

For the single parent, jumping back into the dating scene again is something that will help you develop a new sense of confidence. You need to find the right person with whom you can share some amazing experiences and maybe even start a family. You have been single for almost ten years now, which might make it difficult for you to know where to start in looking for your perfect match. There are different places where you can meet people online or offline that would be interested in dating a single parent. There are also events that are organized that would be a perfect place for you to meet single men or women. If you have a job, you can volunteer to help out at an event. Or maybe your best friends are getting married, and there is no better place for you to meet new people than weddings.

One of the biggest challenges is knowing where to look for someone who will understand your situation as a single mom or dad. It might also be difficult if you want to date someone who has children of their own because they might not want the same thing as you in life. You also need to let go of the idea that you will never find anyone who could love both your children and you. If you look at it as a challenge, it can be something exciting because you will have a chance to put some effort into finding someone else.

You need to keep trying and don't give up on the hope that there is someone out there who wants to spend the rest of their life with you. Try not to get discouraged because this is where being alone becomes your friend in life. It helps you become more comfortable with yourself, and it also helps make life easier when your children leave because single people tend to enjoy their time alone. You should savor every moment of your life and never regret a decision that you have made in this beautiful life that was given to you.

- **Your kid's room and belongings**

Make sure to check the items you put away and make sure that you keep anything that has value to your child. Don't treat your child's bedroom like a shrine. If they leave it in a mess, clear out the clutter and take out the trash.

Your child may want to come back for their things in the future, so make sure not to throw out any important items. Give it back only when they ask for it. If your child never returns for the item, getting rid of it is okay since you don't need it anymore.

You may also want to sell off your kid's old toys and electronics instead of keeping them around, waiting for them to come back for them.

Focus on the positives of your kid moving out. After all, this is their time to grow into adulthood and their time to begin enjoying their life. If you have trouble dealing with empty nesting in the midst of a difficult period in your life, try giving yourself a break from it for the short term by taking a trip or spending some quality time with an old childhood friend.

If you cannot get rid of the feelings of sadness and fear, then write down some notes about what you feel so that you can refer to them when they return. These notes can be used as very useful strategies to deal with these feelings.

You can also use these strategies with your spouse or family members who are also going through empty nesting. Have a plan for what you want to do. If you don't like the feeling of emptiness, make plans for something to do.

Make sure that the schedules that you have set are reasonable so that it does not get in the way of your other obligations. If these new changes in your life interfere with other responsibilities, then it may be best to backtrack and set reasonable goals for yourself.

Take up a hobby or learn something new. Take this opportunity to try out a new activity that you wouldn't normally be able to do if your kids were living at home.

Invite friends and have fun making new memories. Setting healthy boundaries with teens is especially important at this time. You can also set up a "camp" in your house.

Be sure to let them know that you will check on them occasionally; otherwise, leave them alone for two weeks. This will help them get used to living on their own without you constantly in their lives.

Avoid setting unrealistic expectations for your child's behavior if he or she decides to return home after leaving home for college or military service.

If you want to maintain friendships with your child, limit yourself in what you do about your relationship with her. It may be best to allow them to lead this new relationship.

Share your house with your children. If you want kids back in the family home, ensure everyone involved understands and is okay with this decision. If you encourage your child to move back home, do not argue with her or him about moving out and returning.

Work together to find a solution that satisfies everyone's needs as a family and as an individual. Be sure that everyone is on the same page when it comes to your relationship with each other. Space is important for children, but it can be difficult for parents who are used to having their kids around all the time.

There will be more room for other things in your life as you begin to get in the groove of things again without your child there to disrupt everything.

This also gives you more time to create more memories as a family. Create a plan to make new memories with your spouse while the kids are gone. You may not be able to replace your memories of being with your kids, but don't let them be the only reason for living life to its fullest. It can also be helpful if you focus on your spouse as much, if not more, as you did when your kids were home. Make sure that you spend quality time together without distractions to reconnect with each other and heal from the empty-nesting syndrome. Be aware of common empty nesting triggers. You may be entering into a new phase of life that can cause you to become overwhelmed by emotions such as fear, anxiety, or sadness.

If you find yourself losing it when your kids leave home, try to understand what is causing this and what you can do about it. You may be going through a hard time, like the death of a friend or family member or the loss of your job.

You will have to deal with feelings like depression, loneliness, guilt, and resentment if you are not ready for these changes in your life. Consider counseling if things get difficult emotionally for you after your kids leave home.

- **Gradually let go of their messy behaviors.**

Some children tend to retain stencils in their rooms, under the bed, or all over the room. The best way to deal with them is by being understanding and forgiving. Remember that you are the parent, and they are your children; this means that they will eventually do what you want them to do. You should show disapproval of their actions as a parent but make sure not to argue with them because it will not solve anything. If you argue with them, they will argue back, which can lead to emotional outbursts. Now that they have moved out, you can pick up your cups and plates and return them to their rightful places. Enjoy peace of mind since you no longer need to keep checking for such items in their rooms.

You may feel compelled to add items to the room to remind you of your kids. However, adding extra things is unnecessary because you need to be an adult. You can make your own arrangements if you really want to. It's okay to feel this way because it is normal to feel sentimental about your kids' belongings. You can move those items that are not necessary to the storage room.

If you have the urge to do something, you can always remind yourself that they are no longer in the house and will not be back anytime soon.

Your kids may tend to be messy and leave behind a disaster after using the microwave. After they have moved out, you may find yourself staring at the microwave whenever you use it and think about how messy your children used to leave it. You may decide to send them a picture of how clean the microwave remains after you use it.

By now, you're certainly used to being updated on movies by your child, so why stop now? It's also a great way to stay close to your children by staying in touch with what they're watching.

Make sure you are okay with the content and make an effort to communicate your feelings about the movie. You can take advantage of face time to get information from your kids. They may live far away from you, but you can still watch their movies and enjoy them.

- **Embrace the little things you do when you miss your kids**

Loitering around paint swatches at home, daydreaming about repurposing your kid's room, or rearranging the kitchen table where you always had your evening coffee together.

This is a normal thing to do when you miss your child. When you feel these emotions bubbling up, talk to someone. It will help you get in touch with your strong emotions and how those around you can support you through this time.

You can also try to busy yourself with other things that will help keep your mind off of the Empty Nest Syndrome, such as exercise, getting enough sleep, cooking, cleaning up after yourself, or even cleaning up after your family members and making sure things are kept clean for when your kids come back for a visit.

Having long idle weekends may remind you of the busy weekends you used to have with your kids. Sometimes you ended up driving several miles to a soccer tournament; other times, you found yourself cooking dinner for kids and sharing a snack with your kid. You can fill those "empty" weekends by finding a new hobby or joining a few clubs. Check whether you still have time for hobbies and clubs you were in before the kids left the house.

Embrace your new identity as an empty nester. When your kids are little, you may feel like you need to maintain the same schedule that you had when they were younger. That's where an empty nest comes from; You realize that you don't have as much time for yourself anymore, so it just feels like something's been taken away from you.

You may now be yearning to get together with your kids, but remember to be happy with what you have. You may even want your kids to find their "personal best." Take pride in their accomplishments because, at one point or another, you were the same person who was highly motivated after your children had accomplished something.

You might never stop worrying about your kid's safety, no matter how far they are when they move out, but you must take care of your own well-being. If you focus on yourself, you will be surprised at how quickly you will forget about them and go back to your normal selfish-mom mode.

- **Explore new ways to keep in touch with your adult child**

You need to remember that you are their parent, and you have the right to keep them in touch with what's going on in your life.

Schedule a weekly call time with your child to find out how they are doing and let them know how you are as well. Make sure to have conversations about the topics that concern you. If you see that they have a hard time with their first job, ask them if they need any help or if they want to quit. Talk like you would when your child was still living with you. Email or text to share other things you might want to share amid the conversation. You can stay in contact with your kids through little touches, including amusing photos, bible verses, and topics of shared interest.

Adjust your expectations

Don't compare your kids to yourself. Millennials and their siblings may want everything individualized, thus appearing entitled and choosy. They may have a different career concept, which may involve job hopping. They may question everything and not trust systems and institutions. When talking to your children, get a good factual rundown of what is going on in their lives. Remember, the relationship between you and single kids and those who are married will be different. Respect marriage's boundaries and foster a good relationship with your child's spouse.

Show Acceptance

Acceptance plays a crucial role in building healthy relationships with your kids. You can do this by listening to your children, being sensitive, and forgiving them, so they feel they can trust you. Don't blame their choices on their age, what they want or where they want to live. You might feel that you need to be critical just because you are older and wiser but don't forget about the wisdom that comes with fear and love for your child. Parental love does not entail condoning bad behavior, and neither does it mean you accept it. You may have the best intentions in wanting your child to do well, but if driven by anxieties, it can create a feeling of conditioned love.

Think of your kid as a person you would like to be friends with

Developing a meaningful relationship with your grown kids should be your main goal. You should be curious about them and spend time with them. You can enjoy your free time by keeping up with what is going on in your life. Call your kids or visit them in person if you don't have anybody to talk to. At times, you may want to vent out the stress and feelings of insecurity that you feel because of the Empty Nest Syndrome.

Become a good listener

Younger adults can struggle with being heard properly. Encourage them to take a stand for whatever they want in life. It is important not to be too quick to judge but to listen carefully and reflect back on what you hear.

If you have a different stance on the matter, allow your child to express their beliefs instead of expressing your opinions. You should listen carefully and try to see it how they see it, or you can explain things in a way that makes your point clear and simple for the child to understand.

Help yourself, and then accept the change.

Ask your kids to help you learn to be a good friend and parent. You'll both need to be understanding and patient because you will make mistakes. Seek help from professionals.

There are professionals who specialize in helping families and adults with adult children who need help. You can always consult them when you feel like your kids aren't there for you.

Spend time together

Having your kids together is fun, and observing how they interact as adults is always interesting. Invite them for weekend getaways, go to their events, or even enjoy a day of shopping. Don't be afraid to show affection and let them know how proud you are of their accomplishments.

Once a mother, always a mother. Right? However, not quite. This new relationship with your now adult kids changed the way you are as a mother. But hold on a moment. You are much more than a mother, and you are a beautiful woman way before being a mother. The next chapter will help you reconnect with yourself as a person and woman.

Chapter Eight

You are much more than a mother

"When it comes to defining who you are, does it always have to go "mom" first, then "partner" then "friend" or "sister" or "woman"?"

- **Having a child rebuilt your identity as a mother.**

The term mother means different things to different people. Your role as a mother defines your identity so much that it becomes your family's identity and will last forever. You can't escape it when you're in contact with your adult children. Identity reconstruction after having a child is kind of like chewing gum. It stretches to fit the limitations and circumstances of its environment but regains its shape when taken out of the mouth. Self-esteem is the evaluation of oneself in both positive and negative terms.

In many cases, the word mother is used first and foremost as a person's role as a parent. Or it can signify that you are a woman who has given birth to children. In some cultures, women are automatically considered mothers, and in other areas, they are not considered or judged to be "mothers" until they have undergone some ritual of becoming mothers.

Mothering proved you successful.

Despite your accomplishments as a mother, it's hard to know that, in many ways, you are regarded as a failure. This shows how important the role of the mother is. We tend to judge what people have accomplished by what their children have been able to accomplish in life. Our society is geared around motherhood. It's just part of our culture that we expect women to be mothers, and we don't recognize the full spectrum of who they are otherwise. In our society's eyes, every woman must fit into the mold of the mother. We have a hard time allowing women to be independent in any way, and we don't understand that being a mother doesn't need to be your first priority anymore.

Mothering gave you belonging.

Being a mother gave you something you can never give to children ever again. Looking at your child as you would, your mother used to let everyone know that you are a safe person and that they can trust you. If a woman has children, she is automatically regarded in the community as part of the community. Children are raised by their families and not by other people who may be untrustworthy or not be there for them when they need it. All of these things together give meaning and belonging to women's lives, and on many levels, it gives meaning to what being a mother is all about.

A mother is more valued than a wife.

Having children brought you more respect from the men and women in your community. It didn't take away your freedom, but it gave you more respect in a way. In many ways, relationships are based on how much money we make and how much power we have, but having children as a woman gives you more respect as a mother than being wealthy and powerful outside of being a mother.

Mothering made you give up things

Mothering means being a parent that performs the role of her children. A mother is celebrated for caring for her children and being there for them in every way, whether it is taking care of them, loving them, providing them with nutritious meals, or making sure they are safe in terms of health and safety. In some ways, it can be a lot of work to do these things, but your identity as a mother is defined in terms of these things. It may take up some of your time or make you very tired, but the satisfaction you get from doing these things makes all the work worthwhile.

- **You may have had to give up your career.** In many cultures, being a mother is the only performance a woman can be in public. Being a mother isn't simply going to the market and buying groceries. Having children isn't taking care of them from morning to night. It involves getting up at certain times, walking them to school, teaching them things, playing with them, and watching them grow. This is all part of being a mother and takes up much of your time. The days you spend with your kids are not something you would bring your career into, and in many ways, your career is one large distraction for you if you want to be the best mom you can be for your kids.

- **You had less free time as a mother.** Having children takes up most of your time. Once you are a mom, you have less free time to do whatever you want or find time for activities that bring peace or comfort to your life.

- You had less sleeping time. Most children are not at the best of times asleep by themselves. They sleep more during the day when you need to be awake and less when you want to sleep. As a mother, you need a lot of sleep so that your kids can wake up at their proper times and get enough nutrition. Many mothers have to wake up at certain hours to be available for the activities they have with their children.

It is time to rediscover yourself.

Rediscovering yourself when your kids grow up means that you are living your own life differently. You get to be whom you want to be as a person. You are now free of responsibilities and have nothing to do all day. This is not the time to feel that you have lost yourself in your role as a mother. Many women are clueless about who they are and their true interests outside of being a mother. Re-discovering yourself is a way to ensure your true identity doesn't go into hiding and that you return to life again. An empty nest provides a self-rediscovery opportunity by letting go of all the things that have been in your life because you were a mother. You have to make sure you are taking good care of yourself and finding a way to feel happy and fulfilled again in what you do outside of being a wife or mother. You can be who you want to be without being anyone else.

Take care of your looks.

You have to take care of your appearance; this is one of the best things you can do for yourself, even if you are no longer a wife or mother. If you want to be attractive, then dress in attractive clothing and be sure that your hair is always in order. Make sure that your skin always looks flawless and smooth as well. Taking care of yourself will ensure you have higher self-esteem and feel better about yourself overall.

Focus on yourself

You have to focus on yourself and not a bunch of other things that you have to take care of as a mother. Many mothers aren't happy about their life at home because too many things have been left undone, and they feel guilty about these things. Instead, you need to focus on yourself even though you may not have time for the things that used to be your priority before. You need to make sure that you are spending your time in ways that make you feel happy and fulfilled without being anyone else but yourself.

Self-Care Quiz

1. What's the best sleep duration for people above age 40?
   - 7 hours
   - 6 hours
   - 8 hours
   - 9 hours

2. Close friends can reduce stress, boost happiness and help you maintain healthy habits. How many hours do you spend with someone before you form a close friendship?
   - 200 hours
   - 150 hours
   - 70 hours
   - 25 hours

3. What habit can you give up to help you sleep better, feel more energetic and even lose weight?
   - Watching TV
   - Drinking alcohol
   - Drinking Coffee

- Phone scrolling at all hours

4. You can declutter your home to boost your mood. What is not recommended while decluttering?
- Getting it all over in one push
- Working systematically
- Buy one new thing and get rid of one old thing

5. What are three good ways to help your outlook with a positive attitude?
- Finding funny videos to watch when you are angry
- Letting problems resolve themselves
- Fake smiling until it becomes real
- Looking for the silver lining in bad situations

6. What spending do you do for self-care that makes you happiest?
- Spending on new clothes or shoes
- Spending on dining out
- Spending on others
- Spending on fixing up the house

Answers:

1. The most recommend sleep for people over 40 is 7 hours.

2. To form a close friendship, a study at the University of Kansas found that it takes 200 hours.

3. Drinking alcohol is a habit to give up to help you sleep better, feel more energetic, and even lose weight!

4. It is not recommended to declutter your home all at one time. Do it one room or one corner at a time.

5. A positive attitude can help in a lot of situations. Finding funny videos, fake smiling, or looking for the silver lining are all ways to help promote a positive attitude when you are down.

6. Researchers at Harvard University have found that spending money on other people makes people feel the best.

One major difficulty in focusing on yourself and on your healing is the strong feelings that are invading you right now. The next chapter is here to help you embrace, manage, and overcome those hard emotions and reroute yourself toward happiness.

Chapter Nine

Take care of your feelings

"Some people believe holding on and hanging in there are signs of great strength. However, there are times when it takes much more strength to know when to let go and then do it."- Ann Landers

- **It's okay to grieve**

Grieving means letting go of something or someone you once loved by experiencing pain and suffering. Grieving is healthy for the mind and body because it helps you let go of things you hold on to. Even though you may not want to acknowledge your feelings about losing someone or something, grieving will help you deal with the situation healthily without lingering over it too long. You must be supportive during grieving to ensure you let go of things without putting up too much resistance. This will minimize the pain and suffering you may encounter from grieving.

Let yourself go and acknowledge your feelings without putting up a defense or a front. It is better to express your emotions than suppress them and have lingering and painful thoughts in the back of your mind. We may not be able to change what happened or control the environment we are in. We need to acknowledge this and accept that things are the way they are, even though we may not like them. Accepting things as they are doesn't mean you don't want things to be different or won't take action to change them when possible, but it does mean permitting yourself to accept where you are now.

Grieving is a phase in life, and it will pass. You will eventually move on to a new feeling when one ends: happiness, anger, or sadness. It is about letting go and being in the present moment with what you are going through. You may not want to acknowledge your feelings about your child leaving, but grieving does not mean you hold onto feelings for a long time. It means permitting yourself to feel whatever happens to be there. We all have seasons in life where we experience loss and pain. We will experience many joys and happiness, but we must get through the pain and suffering to reach them.

You will feel sad when your children leave home because you will miss those moments when they were young. Allow yourself to go through this phase when the time comes. Grieving is not about going around in circles with your feelings of loss but rather allowing yourself to accept where you are and move on to a better place. There will be many seasons where you can look back on the ones that went by and recall all of the good times. Your children are off doing their own things, but they're still your children and will always be there for you when you need them.

- ## The symptoms of grief

When you grieve, there are good chances you will have grief symptoms. Grief can either result in physical or emotional symptoms. Physical symptoms of grief include headaches, fatigue, insomnia, and loss of appetite. Emotional symptoms include depression, guilt, and loneliness. It is important to understand these symptoms and what they mean so that the pain improves very quickly. If you are experiencing symptoms of grief, it may be beneficial to see a counselor or therapist because they will help you deal with your feelings more healthily. They can help you work through the grieving process so that you accept the empty nest sooner rather than later.

The five stages of grief

The five stages of grief are denial, anger, bargaining, depression, and acceptance.

1. **Denial**: You may deny that you have to deal with this situation. You put off the thought that children are now grown-ups and they have moved out.

2. **Anger**: After denial comes feelings of anger, bitterness, and resentment. You will feel an unrelenting sense of anger and hos-

tility towards the action of your child moving out. You will want revenge on them because they took something away from you that you can never return. This is one of the most difficult stages of grief because you will feel emotionally unstable and unable to control your emotions and actions.

3. **Bargaining**: You will be bargaining with yourself, saying that your children should come back to your house.

4. **Depression**: You mustn't take yourself too seriously while dealing with grief because depression is a common result of grief. You may feel suicidal when you are going through the depression stage because you will feel helpless and hopeless about things again.

5. **Acceptance**: Accepting that things aren't going to get any better or getting used to the feelings of grief is one of the hardest things you have to go through. This will take months, sometimes years, if not for the rest of your life. You will realize that to live a happy life without pain and suffering, you must accept what you have been feeling and move on from there.

Dealing with your grief

A strong support system is one of the best things you can do when grieving. A support system might include your family, friends, and your partner.

These are a few ways you can deal with your grief:

1. Acknowledge your pain: You need to acknowledge that your pain is real, and you shouldn't ignore the things that are making you feel bad. Acknowledging your pain helps to justify it, makes it seem easier to handle, and helps you move through the grief process. You need to take a realistic look at your child leaving and acknowledge that it is an important stage in life.

2. Be kind to yourself: It is important to be kind to yourself and your feelings throughout the grieving process. Being kind to yourself means that you shouldn't avoid or suppress your feelings. Embrace all emotions that you are feeling, including anger, jealousy, regret, and sadness. You will also have to let go of the need to control what has happened. Try not to worry because worrying only prolongs the grieving process.

3. Accept the timing: There is no right or wrong time to grieve. When your child moves out, it can be anytime during the next few months or even years. You will have to accept how long your grief will last based on how deep your pain is and how long it takes you to heal.

4. Look after your body: It is crucial to look after your physical health while going through grief because taking care of your body helps heal the pain in your heart and mind. Taking care of your body is a great way to improve your emotional health as well. You will be glad to know that exercise and eating healthier food can heal your body, so you should eat well and stay active to feel better emotionally.

5. Sleep tight: It is important to remember that taking care of your body will also help you sleep better. It will allow sleep to heal your soul and the world around you. You can spend a little more time sleeping so that you can rest better and allow yourself to heal.

6. Organize your day: While you are going through the grieving process, it is important that you take care of your day. You will want to keep busy with things so that you don't have time to feel sad or depressed. It is important to keep yourself busy because sitting at home and doing nothing will just make you feel worse about yourself and totally worthless. This is why it is important for you to pick up a hobby or interest in your life so that you can focus on something else besides your problems and help other people as well.

7. Talk to your Social Circle: You must talk to someone and be open about your grief. Get to know how your friends are coping with the empty nest and ask for tips. Many people have experienced an empty nest and learned to embrace it; you can learn a lot from them.

8. Find a support group: If you cannot talk to anyone in your family or social circle, you might want to go to a support group for people who have been through the same loss.

9. Start a journal: Writing in a journal is a great way to help you deal with grief and sadness. You can write down your feelings and thoughts to let go of emotions that are stuck inside you. If your grief is because your child has left home, you can express yourself through writing, by writing letters to that person or talking to them. Ultimately, it will heal your soul because it will allow you to release all the negative energy stuck there.

10. Look after your spiritual needs: It is important that you honor your spiritual needs while you are grieving. To help your mind and soul heal, you must get yourself into the right frame of mind. You need to have a positive outlook on life and appreciate what you have. You should also be able to accept the fact that life goes on, and it is important that you do not give up on life because of your loss.

11. **Allow acceptance**: You must allow yourself to accept that your children have moved out. Not only will it help you move on, but it will also help your spouse be more accepting of your situation. You should take advantage of the freedom that results and spend more time with each other.

• **Do I need therapy?**

This book has powerful advice that will help you through your pain. But should you need additional help as you process your feelings, seek therapy.

There are also many support groups for people who have an empty nest. If a support group is not built into your community, do some research on the internet or ask some friends and family members if they know of one.

Over time, the pain will lessen, and eventually, you will accept that your children are capable of their own. There will be an aura of relief surrounding you. Acceptance of their absence has finally arrived.

There are three types of therapy for Empty Nest Syndrome:

1. Individual therapy: The goal of therapy is to help you make sense of your current life, learn how to manage difficult emotions, and adjust to the changes that are necessary because of your child moving out. For example, a therapist might work with you on identifying fears about abandonment or fears about being different from other people. A therapist might also work on finding ways to express and cope with emotions even when no one understands their intensity.

2. Couples therapy: If you are in a relationship, married, or have a partner, it is a good idea for you and your partner to see a therapist. Couples therapy can help you work through the steps of grief and move on with your life.

3. Family counseling: If you are close to your siblings, parents, or children, it might be a good idea to see a therapist or counselor working with a family. Depending on your age and the ages of your family members, therapy can help you adjust to the separation and move forward.

A good therapist will work with you to identify where you are in the grieving process and will encourage you to express your emotions freely as long as they are healthy and helpful. Family counseling may make sense if siblings have different ways of coping: one feels better when everyone gets around each other for meetings or parties; another feels worse when his or her needs for privacy aren't met. A family counselor can help find solutions that work for everyone.

Now that you are able to deal with your hard feelings, it is time to embrace life again. After all, life is here for you to enjoy it. The

THE EMPTY NEST DISCOVER YOUR NEW LIFE FOCUS

next chapter will help you rediscover the joys of life and fall in love with it again.

Chapter Ten

Fall in love with being alive

"The afternoon of life is just as full of meaning as the morning; only, its meaning and purpose are different."- Carl Jung

- **Explore the positives of your new situation**

Focus on some of the positive points of your kids moving out. Maybe you can look at the positive side of things, like you have more time to yourself now that your life is not ruled by their presence, and start planning for the days ahead. Getting through this stage of grief will help you move on and make your way back to life as a whole.

If you find yourself in a rut or someone tries to push you back into the hole of depression, remind yourself that everything is still

THE EMPTY NEST DISCOVER YOUR NEW LIFE FOCUS

up for grabs in the second half of your life. Remember, life is filled with more than just the loss of a loved one. It's filled with countless opportunities and adventures that await us every day.

Enjoy the economic advantages.

The contemporary academic literature on ENS assumes that its existence is the result of social change and economic forces, especially the aging of the boomers and the shift to a post-industrial economy. But it's also important to appreciate how its existence can accelerate these changes. It takes time to get used to living alone – making meals by yourself, and deciding how to spend your time every day. Going through this process forces people to accept their new status in life, which can lead them (either immediately or after several years) to make choices that are more consistent with their current situation.

Downsize your home

If you have a larger home, consider downsizing it instead. Start by paring down household chores and figuring out which ones are just not worth doing. Then, take the rest of your family members on home tours to help you decide where their rooms should go.

When downsizing, don't let the outside appearance of your house determine its functionality. Keep certain things that are important to you – such as a large-screen TV and a swimming pool – while deciding what should go into storage instead. Understand that certain elements of the house are linked with feelings of loss – so parting with them will be difficult as well. Deciding how much is enough has more value than how big is too much.

Go back to the passions you gave up.

What were your passions before having kids? Your hobbies? Your interests? Your career? Maybe the things that kept you going in the past weren't for you anymore. Maybe you had to let go of them just to make room for the family, but now it's time to return to them. We have a saying: "You don't have time for everything." Letting go of things that used to be important to you will free up some of your life and allow more time for what is still important – whether it be spending more uninterrupted hours with your children or working on a new project.

Discover new interests

It's easy to fall into the rut of accepting your life because it's what you have always had. If you have to have a "normal" life, let yourself get a little crazy. Find a hobby that delights you – whether it's drawing, painting, gardening, or embroidery – and do it until your fingers are ready to fall off. Keep doing it once or twice a week – regardless of if anyone in your family is interested in watching or participating. You can always trade activities with someone else at some point down the road, but right now, what you want most is to spend uninterrupted hours enjoying an activity that doesn't require anyone else in the family's participation.

Ask questions that move you forward.

Your kids aren't the only ones who are moving away – there is likely a great deal of movement in your own life as well. You are moving from the family to the empty nest, from one occupation to another, from married life to single life (again). When you ask yourself where you want to be in a year and five years, visualize it and let it be perfect. Be sure you ask yourself questions along the way that keep you on track with your plans. If you're not where you want to be a year from now, keep re-evaluating and adjusting until you are truly happy with your life. You need to devise a plan, stick to it and ensure that you are still on track for the future.

Cover all areas of your life

You need to become more active in other areas of your life. Attend parties, join clubs and organizations you have always wanted to be a part of, listen to new music, try new foods and do something that doesn't involve the kids every day. Do these things for yourself because you deserve any bit of fun or enjoyment you can get.

An essential part of enjoying life is having others around you to share those joys with. The next chapter focuses on your relationships and helps you become surrounded once more by friends whose company you enjoy.

Chapter Eleven

Renew your friendships or make new ones

"We need old friends to help us grow old and new friends to help us stay young." – Letty Cottin Pogrebin

- **Having children made your friendships suffer.**

Your focus on relationships and friendships was diminished as a result of having a child. This is because the nurturing relationship between a parent and a child requires time, energy, and attention. Sometimes this bonding process can be so intense that it could have the same effect as losing someone.

Therefore, when your children are older, and you feel like your life is beginning to return to normal, then it's time for you to get out there and meet new people. It might be toward a new career or work, but it might not; meet with other people who share common interests in your local community through hobby classes, sports, or activities that your kids do. Put yourself back into the world of friends, not just family.

Talk to your empty-nester friends.

An empty nester's relationships with their friends change as they move through life stages, but the dynamics of their relationships with other boomer parents change little. They have already figured out the fundamental issues of raising their kids, so they have time and energy to do other things. When you talk to them about the new challenges in your life, ask them for suggestions about how to deal with them or help with a problem that is unrelated to your children.

Renew old friendships

Some friendships diminished or died due to having children, so you may want to renew them and explore what such friendships offer. You both might want to start fishing together again or going out to the movies together. You might both like to continue your work with a volunteer organization or get together with some friends for lunch once in a while. You might participate in an art club or join an exercise class so you can meet different people without children around.

Start a group for things that interest you.

Find or start a group for people who share your interests, such as needle-crafting, playing cards, or learning foreign languages. You can also start an organization, such as an adult education class that meets in the evening once a week at the community center, library, or church. Your new friends will understand you are no longer available during most of the day to socialize with them, and you can easily establish new friendships your own way. Spending time with people who have similar interests will help increase your self-esteem and help you feel better about yourself. This will improve your life, relationships with other people, and productivity.

Where to meet new friends

Meeting new friends does not have to be hard. Try joining a club or organization which is related to your interest area. While doing so, you will be able to meet people who share the same interest as you do and may become friends with these people. Here are a few tips for making new friends:

1. Go to places where you meet people regularly: Parties and social gatherings are great places to meet new people. You may also meet new friends when you visit museums, art galleries, concerts, theater performances, and more. Check out your local community calendar to find out what special events are available in your area.

2. Do not decline invitations: When you are invited to a party or event, go and meet as many people as possible. Get involved in conversations with the people around you. Make sure that you socialize and have fun during the event. You will have more chances of meeting new people if you are enjoying yourself at the party.

3. **Take advantage of the value of small talk:** Small talk will help you build rapport with other people. Try to make a positive first impression on others and be friendly to everyone.

Make friends online

There are several apps you can use to make friends online. They include Hey VINA, Friender, and Next door.

1. Hey, VINA: This app is great if you want fun. You should download Hey VINA, and it will help you connect with new people by adding them to your Facebook friend list.

2. Friender: This app is free, easy to use, and great for connecting with new people worldwide, so you can chat with your friends about the same activities you do.

3. Next Door: First off, this app is free and looks like a photo-sharing site with a group of people in your local area who are in the same groups as you. It's also easy to use and has various group types, from sports teams and businesses to volunteer groups or movie nights.

Another essential part of yourself you had to sacrifice for your children was your career. You may have dropped out of college without finishing your degree or let go of that promotion you have always wanted to be able to give them the time and attention they needed. You may even have always dreamed of learning something but had to wait until a more suitable time. Well, there is no time better than now to learn and improve your career. The next chapter will help you make it happen.

Chapter Twelve

Improve your career

"It's not only children who grow. Parents do, too. As much as we watch to see what our children do with their lives, they are watching us to see what we do with ours. I can't tell my children to reach for the sun. All I can do is reach for it, myself."- Joyce Maynard

Here are ways you can improve your career:

1. Learn a craft: If you want to increase your net worth and income, I suggest learning a craft. This requires knowledge, hard work, and cost. But the benefits are far more than monetary.

2. Learn a new language: It can open doors in business and make you more marketable among the foreign population.

3. Take free or reduced tuition courses online: Open education resources are courses that are free to take from your home. Courses are available on a wide range of topics, including health care, computer and Internet skills, language translations, and even hobbies. Usually, these courses provide a certificate at the end. Take advantage of these resources and reduce the cost of your education.

4. Develop your career with online university courses: Online courses provide lower tuition costs and easier access than traditional classes. These courses offer a range of options for adult learners who desire college degrees without the time and expense of on-campus classes. You can explore MOOC courses, which offer free online classes, explore degree programs and take a few classes to see if you like them. If you decide to pursue a degree and prefer hands-on experience, you can complete a degree with an online campus program.

5. Go back to college: As an adult learner, you can go back to college. Your options include traditional campus-based programs, online campus programs, and online university courses. The USA has various adult learning centers available such as:

- **Shepherd's centers:** Located in the south, they provide learning opportunities for the retired population. Shepctrg.org

- **OASIS**: Adult education programs are offered to adults aged 50 years and over. It is a resource for lifelong learning and community education. Oasisnet.org

6. Start your own business: As an entrepreneur, you are the key to your business' success. That is why you must learn how to manage your time and money effectively if you want to succeed.

Online learning is a great way to gain practical knowledge, develop or enhance skills, or pick up a new hobby for free.

Personal growth will be complete only if you make a good balance in your life. The next chapter will help you fill your life with things that can give it more purpose and meaning.

Chapter Thirteen

Fill Your Life With Meaningful Things... Especially if You're Single

"Life isn't about finding yourself. Life is about creating yourself."- George Bernard Shaw

In order to live a meaningful life, you can do the following:

1. Make a list of all the things you couldn't do: such as learn to play an instrument, coach a sport, make a film, or travel the world. Look at what you can do: start dance classes, volunteer for Habitat for Humanity, and go hiking. Take action on your list. It doesn't have to be involved in each thing on your list. You can just take small baby steps toward achieving something.

2. **Enjoy your "on your own" time:** You don't have to do anything or have anything planned each day. Just make sure you have had a good night's sleep and wake up refreshed each morning. Get out of the house, go to the park or just walk around in a new place. Your body is designed to move and explore its surroundings. It keeps you healthy, vibrant, and alive.

Spending quality time by yourself is crucial, especially when you are going through a hard time. You can reflect or have alone time. You can clear your head and think about the things that are important to you, your goals, and what you want to do in life.

3. **Keep a gratitude journal:** Every day, dedicate time to write down three things that you're thankful for. No matter how big or small your life is, there will always be times when you are happy, and things are going well. Buy a new journal and get yourself a pen. See what you can come up with. This will help you keep things in perspective and ensure that you're not taking anything for granted. Use visual reminders on your refrigerator, such as postcards or even pictures. It makes it easier to remember what you're grateful for.

4. **Adopt a pet:** Everyone needs a pet. You can choose from thousands of pets, from hamsters to dogs to snakes. Adopting a pet gives you something to do in your free time and a constant companion. This will help you not feel lonely and provides emotional support and unconditional love. Pets are also a therapeutic way to keep your stress levels low.

5. Read the books you missed: Find a comfortable spot, pour your cup of hot chocolate and start reading the books you want to read. Take a break and find inspiration in authors who have been there and done it. They will teach you how to take that leap of faith, how to travel the world, live in a different city, or just how to change your life.

6. Write: Start a journal and write about everything you feel. It doesn't have to be fancy, just an honest account of your thoughts and feelings. When you finish your journal entry, read through it again. This will help you to stop and reflect on your life, especially when things are not going well.

7. Binge on a new tv show: If you're not sure what to do in your binge-watching free time, watch a new tv show. Get yourself hooked up with a new series that you can watch over and over again. You will forget about all the bad things in your life and enjoy some good times with the characters of your favorite tv show.

8. Re-organize your space for your comfort: This may not seem exciting, but it will give you a sense of control and bring more peace of mind into your life. Find your favorite music and start singing in the shower; you can do anything to make yourself feel good. If you have boxes that are not being used, throw them out, put another layer of paint on the walls or organize your spice rack.

9. Try new Cuisine: Find a new recipe for your favorite food and make it for yourself. You will spend your time doing something useful, and cooking your own food will make you so proud that you did it all by yourself. Try to cook new dishes, even if you're not sure if they will taste good! You can never go wrong with trying new things.

10. Volunteer: Make a new commitment and put your time and effort into something you believe in. It doesn't have to be that hard if you don't have the money to donate. Figure out how to make a positive change in yourself or those around you, whether it is helping someone less fortunate or volunteering for whatever cause you want to support. You will feel giving and efficient at the same time.

11. Connect on social media: Facebook, Twitter, Instagram, and other social media can be great tools for connecting yourself with others. It is easier than ever to make new friends with the help of social media.

12. Start gardening: Plant something that grows from seeds, and keep it alive till the end of the week. Take good care of it, water it every day, and see how your little plant will grow. This is a great way to connect with nature and a mini exercise.

13. Explore music: If you're an artist, try to find a new creative outlet. If you are not, listen to music that inspires you, whether it's your favorite band or a song you've never heard before. Go to a musical concert and take in the atmosphere. If you are not into concerts, just listen to your favorite songs on repeat and see if they have helped you create anything in your life.

14. Update your wardrobe: Clean out your closet and drawers. Throw away anything that you don't wear anymore, and bring in some new pieces for your wardrobe. Find yourself a new pair of jeans, shoes, or simple accessories and wear them at work, out with friends, or just for going to the grocery store. It will make you feel good about who you are, what you wear, and how it makes you look.

15. Spend some time with kids: Take an hour out of your week and spend time with a child. Whether it is taking a walk with a child, reading them a bedtime story, or just playing games around the house, you will feel great after spending quality time with them.

16. Restart dating: Get back to work if you have been in a long-term relationship or are single and fed up with the dating scene. You need to put yourself out there and ask someone out on a date. You don't have to be stuck in the same routine you're unhappy with. Start moving forward and try to make some new friends. Maybe it will be your chance at love, or maybe it just makes you happy; either way- you're winning!

After the kids flew away, you found yourself with your partner on your own. All the things that you have been putting off to tend to your children's needs are resurfacing now. The next two chapters will help you enjoy being together again as the happy couple you once were.

Chapter Fourteen

Who is that man?

Tony and Jane used to dream about what it would be like when their children left home. They imagined they would do the things they used to do before they had kids. Tony and Jane worked hard to put their kids through college. Jane took extra shifts as a labor and delivery nurse, while Tony took every home remodeling job he could. Whenever they had time together, they spent it talking about the kids. By the time their kids moved out, Tony and Jane were so busy that they didn't have time for each other. Jane was the first to feel lonely with the kids gone. When Tony came home, his primary focus was on the TV. This wasn't the life after kids they had dreamed about.

- **Don't lose your partner too**

The divorce rate among couples aged 55-64 has more than doubled since 1990. Couples struggle to remember the fun things they did together before they had kids. Many couples spend so much effort raising children that reconnecting later becomes difficult.

THE EMPTY NEST DISCOVER YOUR NEW LIFE FOCUS

When the children leave and both parents no longer share the mission of taking care of them, it becomes hard to manage the transition.

It's just you and me now.

Reveling in an empty nest often means facing some less-than-pleasant realities, such as being alone with a partner you may not enjoy spending time with. Many people have difficulty coping with emotional changes, which can be difficult for one person to handle. This is where couples therapy can help. It can help you and your partner to rediscover how it feels to be together.

For many couples, it takes them over a year after the children start leaving home before they are ready to rediscover each other. The transition between being alone and being together can be difficult, but it will improve.

You will live longer... Together

The empty nest gives you time to bond with your partner. A recent study from the University of Pittsburgh found that older couples who are still in love live three years longer than those who aren't. It took couples two years to get close again after their last child left home. The transition is complicated and is a topic for couple therapy. This transition may also be due to the Empty Nest Syndrome and subsequent depression many parents experience when their children leave home.

Be patient with your partner.

Getting used to being together again will take time. The empty nest may make you feel too old to do the same things you did before the kids left home. This may cause you to lose confidence in what you can do with your partner. If this happens, start by doing things that are easy for both of you and slowly work your way up to more challenging activities. Remember that you're both going through the same transition and may need some time before you fully adjust. Don't be so hard on yourself; get some rest, and accept that things are changing.

- **What if empty nesting shows we are not okay?**

The empty nest may lead you to discover lifelong issues you've had with your partner. If you have unresolved issues, talk about them. It's important to acknowledge your partner's concerns and to be open about your own. Consider working with a family therapist to help you work through these issues. The more time you spend together after the kids move out, the more you'll learn about each other and how to better deal with one another. Take a look at some of the red flags that may indicate your relationship is not in a good state. Signs may include a lack of trust, one partner attempting to control the other, and you feeling uncomfortable addressing your needs and wants to your partner. A lot can be done to strengthen the bond, and you will discover it in this chapter and the next.

Small gestures count more than big ones.

Your partner may feel that your relationship has suffered because of your focus on the kids. This doesn't mean that you've let anyone down or that you don't love your partner. Your relationship will come back if you work at it, but it does mean that the two of you need to make time for each other and prioritize it. When the kids leave home, take a class together or join a club. Don't just spend all your free time catching up on sleep. Here are some creative ways to spend more time together:

- **Plan a dinner date every week** - The dinner date can be as simple as going out to have dinner and talking about your day.

- **Go out on double dates** - You can go out with your partner's family or take a friend along. Have fun with it and return to your relationship's good parts.

- **Take a cooking class together** - This can be simple, like going to the library and picking up a cookbook. You can also plan a romantic night in, spending time with each other while cooking dinner. Sometimes going out to eat is just too much of a hassle and takes away from quality time together.

Be present, not around.

You need to be emotionally and physically present for your partner. We are constantly distracted by our cell phones and more. Try to be present when you are with your partner. This may mean turning off your cell phone so that you're not getting messages or calls at inappropriate times and checking out what is happening around you. It's easy to get distracted by noise and kids, so giving each other your undivided attention is important.

If you are religious, pray together.

Couples who strive to nourish their spiritual relationship have a stronger connection. Faith plays a big part in your life, and this can be an opportunity to improve your relationship. It can help you get closer to your partner by spending time together and thinking about each other. Many couples experience a divide when it comes to faith, so this is where you can have some meaningful discussions with your partner and grow closer as a couple. Prayer can be a time to ask for guidance and healing in your relationship.

Work on communication

Communication can be a challenge in many relationships. It's easy to neglect this part of your relationship if you have a busy schedule or are occupied with the kids. You may feel that you're too tired to talk to your partner or don't want to upset them by bringing something up. If you decide that it needs to be discussed, make sure your partner is ready for this. Whether you have issues with your partner, talk about them so that they can be addressed. For example, you tell your spouse, "I feel ignored when you spend your time watching TV when we are together, and I need you to talk to me about your day."

Rebuilding communication streams

• **Exercise 1. Active listening**: Each partner should list three things they want in their relationship. The other partner should pay attention to understand your partner's needs appropriately.

• **Exercise 2. I hear you:** Repeat what your partner says, starting with, I heard you say.

- **Exercise 3. I see your point of view:** Getting your partner to agree with you is not a must. Listen to your partner respectfully and aim at adequately understanding what they are trying to communicate.
- **Exercise 4. I feel loved by you:** Sit and have a dialogue. Tell your partner I feel loved by you when...(You then tell them what makes you feel loved).
- **Exercise 5. Make it a habit:** Organize a weekly meeting for discussing conflicts as well as the good gestures of your partner within the week. For every complaint, raise five positive attributes.

As this moment in your life is a time to enjoy life, why not enjoy it with your significant other? The next chapter will help you renew the old flame that joins you together through enjoying life in togetherness and growing your intimacy.

Chapter Fifteen

Making a life together

"I love you without knowing how, or when, or from where, I love you directly without problems or pride: I love you like this because I don't know any other way to love, except in this form in which I am not nor are you, so close that your hand upon my chest is mine, so close that your eyes close with my dreams." Pablo Neruda, "One Hundred Love Sonnets: XVII" from The Essential Neruda: Selected Poems

- **Taking your liberties in your home again**

You may be married, but you are still the same person. When was the last time you were comfortable in your home? When was the last time you could watch a movie until the early morning hours or sleep on the couch without being woken up by the kids? You can yell and have parties, and there is no one to have to make a good example for.

Dream along with your partner

Create new routines and goals that you want to work toward together. Your partner is important to you, and you're going to want him or her to be part of your new life. Make sure that your dreams and goals are something that the two of you can work towards together. If you do not agree with what your partner wants, this can cause some issues between you. Little things like going on vacation or buying a new car are things that both partners should want. Try to make sure that the things you are working toward are things that you both agree on.

Care for your love

Use the love language that suits your partner best. What are love languages? The five love languages are words of affirmation, acts of service, receiving gifts, physical touch, and quality time. Each language is different, so you must know your partner's main love language. If a person enters a relationship and their partner's primary love language is not being spoken, you might expect the relationship to be in trouble. When you find out your spouse's primary love language, it just takes some adjustment to build a closer relationship.

Say, "I love you."

We live in a busy world where we don't spend time saying "I love you" or "thank you." Your partner will probably tell you that they love you, but do you really know if you love your partner the way you should? Often, people aren't able to appreciate their partners for how they really are. If your partner is emotionally needy or needy with their physical appearance, then it's up to you to tell them how much they mean to you. When couples open up about what is going on in their lives and communicate through words and actions, it can become easier to talk about finances, children, and other issues.

Light the old flame

Be romantic. You have been busy with work, bills, and the kids, and you have had no time to spend on just yourself. Now is the time to finally make time for the two of you again. Get out of the house for a night and reconnect with your partner by doing something you enjoy together. If you've forgotten what it's like to be in love, then now's the time to remember what it was like back then. For some people, this could be a great opportunity for both of you to get re-fired and remember how good it can feel.

Travel together

Traveling can be a great way to reconnect with your partner. Couples who travel together are less likely to experience divorce than those who don't. Traveling allows you to escape the stress of life on a daily basis and just enjoy each other's company. If you've had an argument or have been having issues lately, this is the time to get away from it all and enjoy your time together as husband and wife.

Go camping

Camping can be a great way to bring back the closeness in your relationship. It allows you to escape for one night. Camping is not just about sleeping on the ground and eating food. If you want it to be romantic, add some candles, wine, and music playing in the background and your favorite blankets. This helps to create a romantic atmosphere that helps both of you feel relaxed. You can talk and laugh more while sitting around the campfire.

Share intense emotions together.

Share all of the things that you are feeling with your partner. Don't try to hide your feelings from them; this could cause an argument later. If you're having a hard time talking about the fact that you're having marital problems and how to fix them, talk about them with your partner as if they were just sitting there next to you. It might be hard at first because you might have to go over some very painful and emotional things, but it's better than being miserable on your own and not addressing it at all.

Start a club group

One thing that you could do is to start a club group. If your partner is a sorority or fraternity member, then this could be something you can do together. You both will have the same interest, bringing you closer as husband and wife. You can also try applying for a club or joining one together. Many couples find co-curricular activities they share or look forward to going to during their downtime. Couples need to maintain some level of interest outside the relationship in order for them to feel fulfilled and happy in their marriage.

Do some physical activity together.

Physical activity is great to do when you are stressed. Couples who can exercise together while doing things they both enjoy are most likely to bond. There are sports that both spouses enjoy, and doing them together can be a great way to connect. When you're working out together, talk about something you will see in the future or something that can make you happy. This could be something as simple as planning a picnic or getting your kids involved with the hobby. If your families have lived in different places, this provides an opportunity for your partner and you to become closer again.

Make a regular date night.

Making a regular date night just like you used to back in the day is great for couples who are trying to keep their relationship going. Make it something that you both look forward to, such as going to dinner and a movie or playing a game of ping pong together. Not only will this help bring your relationship closer, but it will also build some trust and communication.

As you may have found in your reading so far, giving purpose, meaning, and joy to your life is entirely in your hands. The next chapter will help you with tools that can boost your goals of being happy again.

Chapter Sixteen

Look after your personal well-being

> "Be willing to be with yourself as you are with love and compassion."
> - Cheryl Jones. Founder, The Mindful Path

- **Do I actually need to become active?**

How active do I have to be? Trying to fit in physical activities can be difficult with a busy schedule. To get started, have a plan. It can be anything from actual physical exercise like playing a sport or walking to simply going out and shopping or meeting friends. It isn't as much the activity as being active. Being active improves present and future mental health.

It's time to think about exercising.

The empty nest provides an opportunity to exercise, and you should maximize it. Exercise boosts energy levels, reduces stress, increases mood, and helps you sleep better at night. If you're exercising well and keeping yourself active, you'll feel more optimistic and live a healthier life.

Benefits of physical activity

Physical activity adds a lot of benefits to your life. It can help you lose weight, and feeling good about yourself is great. Also, it increases heart rate, lowers blood pressure, and improves sleep quality. Exercise also keeps your joints and muscles moving smoothly. Studies have shown that exercising helps with mental health as well; people who exercise are less likely to suffer from depression or develop dementia later on in life than those who don't keep active.

Have a balanced diet

Ensuring that you have proper nutrition can help prevent major health problems. A healthy diet is beneficial in the long run. Make sure you consume various food daily to keep your body functioning at its best. Get plenty of fiber, and don't skip meals, as this can lead to low metabolism.

Benefits of a healthy diet

Eating healthy is one thing that helps you get in shape, lose weight and improve your overall health and well-being. An active lifestyle is a big part of making you healthier. Here are some benefits of eating a healthy diet:

- Being physically active and getting proper nutrition allows you to feel good about yourself. You will also look great!
- A healthy diet is good for your cardiovascular system, which gives you energy and keeps your body going when it needs it most.

- People who eat a balanced diet see better results in the gym or any other physical activity, as they will have more energy to keep going at their goal. Having a healthy diet also prevents you from feeling exhausted or out of breath, which is helpful when exercising. Eating a balanced diet is also good for your skin and gives you more self-confidence.
- You will have better mental health if you eat various foods. A healthy diet reduces the chances that adult-onset diabetes or heart disease will be detected early.

Harvest the benefits of breathing

Breathing techniques will help you connect with your body, mind, and spirit. It will help you to stay balanced. When we're breathing properly, our bodies are in rhythm, and we feel great! Breathe properly; it is an important sign to see that someone is feeling good and happy.

Prepare your posture

Posture is important. Your overall posture helps you feel better and look better. It makes you more confident when your posture is good. Many times, it is said that we eat with our eyes.

There are various postures you can adopt, including:

- Stand straight with a nice posture and keep your head level.
- Sit up straight with your shoulders back, chest open, and chin up. – (This will increase blood flow to your brain.)
- Keep one hand in front of you on the table or desk to act as a counterweight if it feels like you're falling backward or forwards.

- If you can't sit up straight, try to keep your shoulders back and chest open.

Start breathing

Breathing must follow a certain sequence for it to be effective. You can use the following steps:
- Inhale 1-3 times through the nose.
- Breathe out all the air you take in.
- As you inhale, try to deepen your breath and be sure to exhale.
- Alternate between inhaling and exhaling.
- On your exhalation, try to relax as much as possible and make it slow and deep.
- When practicing this technique, switch from inhaling through the nose to exhaling out of the mouth each time. However, for beginners, it is recommended that you use air from your nose each time.

Practice mindfulness

Mindfulness is a great technique that can help you in everything you do. It can help you connect with your body, mind, and spirit, the three parts of self. You need to be mindful when it comes to eating, exercising, walking, and anything else you do. Being mindful is a way to be active when being active seems impossible. When you're mindful, you'll feel more grateful for everything in life and have more positive thoughts as well. You will take care of yourself, your feelings, and those around you.

Meditate

Meditation is a great tool for helping you in your daily life. It allows you to calm your mind and body, gives you a better state of being, and improves your life overall. The following are some benefits of meditation:

- It helps us understand who we are and what we want from our lives, both physically and mentally.
- When we meditate, we're using our awareness to find the present moment rather than being lost in thought or anticipating what may happen in the future.
- It helps us live a happy and fulfilled life by taking care of ourselves so that we feel good about ourselves during our entire lifetime.
- We become mindful of how to treat others with respect, kindness, and love.

Enjoy life

Enjoying life is one of the best things you can do. When you enjoy life, you stop worrying about things that don't matter and start being happy with what you have. Also, when you're happier, your body is happier!

Leave a 1-Click Review!

I hope you have received at least one good piece of comfort out of this book. If you could leave a review on Amazon and give me your feedback, that would be great.

There is a link or a QR code below to help take you to the right place.

That is, of course, how we grow and move forward.

Have an awesome day.
https://geni.us/ReviewYourPurchases

THE EMPTY NEST DISCOVER YOUR NEW LIFE FOCUS

Review Your Purchases

Conclusion

"It is not what you do for your children, but what you have taught them to do for themselves that will make them successful human beings."-Ann Landers.

The empty nest can be a scary and lonely time. Know that you are not alone. Children moving out of the house is part of the natural family cycle. It is time to let go and let your children become adults. It is a transition. Take the time you need to process the change but know it will get better. Make sure you remember that you are much more than just a mother. You need to fall in love with yourself again, so you are in a place for others to do the same.

The one thing your kids do not want to see is you unhappy and suffering from Empty Nest Syndrome. They Love you. They will feel guilty for living their lives because of how you are feeling. This will hold them back. So... for the sake of your kids and for your own, start auctioning the advice you read in this book today.

"Start by doing what's necessary; then do what's possible; and suddenly you are doing the impossible." – Francis of Assisi.

THE EMPTY NEST DISCOVER YOUR NEW LIFE FOCUS

Take the time to renew old friendships or make new ones. Your life revolved around your children for the last 18-20 years. It is time for you to take it back. Make career choices that were put on hold because you had children. Take some classes and study something you really want to. Start that new job, change careers, get that degree you always wanted, or start a business. Pick up a hobby for you. Crochet, knit, walk, adopt a dog, read a book, write a book, watch a television show you have missed, cook. The possibilities are endless. Do something you really want to. This is your time.

It is also a great opportunity for parents to strengthen their relationships with their partners. Take advantage of this opportunity. Make a regular date night and get to know each other again. Remember why you fell in love in the first place. Plan that dream vacation and actually go. Figure out the best of what you had and the best of what is yet to come.

Look into activities that interest you. Do you like sports, like softball or tennis? How about long-distance walking or horseback riding? Find new or old activities and get involved. Your children now have their own lives. They will visit and ask you to babysit off and on, but you need to fill your days with your own activities. You need to keep active and busy.

"Life isn't about finding yourself. Life is about creating yourself." — George Bernard Shaw.

An empty nest is a great time to learn about yourself and how you can improve your life. Your body, mind, and spirit will thank you for it. When you feel good about yourself, enjoying life will be much easier. The health benefits of a healthy lifestyle will help you in the long run. So, begin today and make your life filled with healthy and enjoyable activities.

Also By Dani Lai MacGregor

Please click on the link or use the QR code below to see other books you'll love!

https://geni.us/AlsobyDaniLaiMacGregor

AlsoByDaniLaiMacGregor

Resources

Stabiner, Karen. "The Empty Nest." *31 Parents Tell the Truth About Relationships, Love, and Freedom After the Kids Fly the Coop*, 2007. *Bowker*, https://doi.org/10.1604/9781401302573.

Hanson, Pam, and Barbara Andrews. *Empty Nest*. Ideals Publications, 2012.

Duffy, Carol Ann. "Empty Nest." *Poems for Families*, Picador, 2022.

Dodd, Celia. "The Empty Nest." *Your Changing Family, Your New Direction*, Piatkus Books, 2011.

Dodd, Celia. "The Empty Nest." *Your Changing Family, Your New Direction*, Piatkus Books, 2011.

Dodd, Celia. "The Empty Nest." *Your Changing Family, Your New Direction*, Piatkus Books, 2011.

Watson, Sue. *The Empty Nest*. 2019.

"The Empty Nest." *When Children Leave Home*, 1995. *Bowker*, https://doi.org/10.1604/9780044408987.

Fitzpatrick, Elyse. "The Empty Nest." *Finding Hope in Your Changing Job Description*, 2012.

Fenwicke, Rosy. *Empty Nest*. 2022.

Palmer, Fiona. *The Empty Nest*. E-Penguin, 2014.

"Empty Nest." *Looking Into the Nest and Beyond*, vol. 3,000, 2014.

Empty Nest. Illustrated by Rumiko Takahashi, 1997. *Bowker*, https://doi.org/10.1604/9781569311554.

Dodd, Celia. "The Empty Nest." *How to Survive and Stay Close to Your Adult Child*, Piatkus Books, 2012.

Cadell, Elizabeth. *The Empty Nest*. 1986.

McEntire, Vickie. *Empty Nest*. Illustrated by Sandy Dutton, 2017.

McEntire, Vickie. *Empty Nest*. Illustrated by Sandy Dutton, 2017.

Avari, Josi. "Empty Nest." *Aloha Chicken Mysteries*, 2020.

"Empty Nest." *Strategies to Help Your Kids Take Flight*, 2014.

Cadell, Elizabeth. *The Empty Nest*. 2019.

Palmer, Fiona. *The Empty Nest*. E-Penguin, 2014.

Menter, Anne Meckstroth. "Empty Nest." *One Mother's Journey*, 2006. *Bowker*, https://doi.org/10.1604/9781425710835.

Bovey, Shelley. "The Empty Nest." *When Children Leave Home*, 2016.

Day, Sandy. "An Empty Nest." *A Summer of Stories*, 2019.

Miller, Frederic P., et al., editors. *Empty Nest*. 2010.

Neukam, Amanda. *Empty Nest*. 2017.

Made in United States
Troutdale, OR
08/08/2023